ADIRONDACK CANOE WATERS

SOUTH AND WEST FLOW

ADIRONDACK CANOE WATERS

SOUTH AND WEST FLOW

Alec C. Proskine

Including the 3 main watersheds of the southern Adirondacks —
the Black, the Mohawk, and the Upper Hudson —
plus the 2 major streams of the Tug Hill Plateau.

The Adirondack Mountain Club, Inc.
Glens Falls, New York
1985

To water lovers, pure water,
pure air, good life everywhere.

Published by the Adirondack Mountain Club, Inc.
172 Ridge Street, Glens Falls, New York 12801

Copyright© 1984 Adirondack Mountain Club, Inc.

Printed and bound in the United States of America

The AWA Safety Code and Classification of Difficulty are from the American Whitewater
Affiliation and are used with permission.

Library of Congress Cataloging in Publication Data

Proskine, Alec C.
  Adirondack canoe waters,

  "Including the 3 main watersheds of the southern Adirondacks—the Black, the
Mohawk, and the Upper Hudson—plus the 2 major streams of the Tug Hill Plateau."
  Bibliography: p.
  Includes index.
  1. Canoes and canoeing—New York (State)—Adirondack Mountains—Guide-books.
  2. Canoes and canoeing—New York (State)—Tug Hill—Guide-books. I. Title.
  GV776.N72A346 1984   917.47'53   84—18616
  ISBN 0-935272-23-2

Note from the Publisher

Paul Jamieson's *Adirondack Canoe Waters — North Flow*, first published in 1975 and now in its second edition, left three of the five Adirondack basins uncovered: the Black River Basin (West Flow) and the Mohawk and Upper Hudson basins (South Flow). The requirements for preparing a companion guide to North Flow were formidable: Needed were a facile writer; an enthusiastic canoeist; leisure time to do the scouting, background study and writing; and, ideally, residence near the rivers to be covered.

In Alec Proskine we found all of these qualifications and more. In a letter to the publisher in May 1980 Paul Jamieson wrote, "It seems to me Alec Proskine is just the person to do South Flow. His training and work as a forester are valuable assets to bring to a study of Adirondack rivers. His writing as evidenced in his *No Two Rivers Alike* is clear, plain, accurate and is enlivened by anecdotes of personal experience on the rivers he describes. He is an experienced canoeist on a wide variety of waters and has the help of a group of active paddlers. I'm glad to hear that he is willing to go ahead with this book."

Together, *Adirondack Canoe Waters — North Flow* and *Adirondack Canoe Waters — South and West Flow* cover the Adirondack Park and the Tug Hill region of northern New York State. The Adirondack Mountain Club is pleased to be the publisher of these two definitive volumes.

CONTENTS ·

Preface ix
AWA Safety Code xii
River Signals xvi
River Difficulty xviii
Flow Chart xix

BOREAS RIVER 1
CEDAR RIVER 5
EAST CANADA CREEK 11
FISH CREEK 18
   East Branch 19
   West Branch 26
HUDSON RIVER 27
   Sanford Lake to Newcomb 27
   Newcomb to Indian River Junction 31
   Hudson River Gorge and Indian River 32
   North River to Hadley Luzerne 36
INDIAN RIVER 43
   Indian Lake 44
   Lewey Lake 44
KUNJAMUK RIVER 50
MOOSE RIVER 54
   Fulton Chain of Lakes 54
   Middle Branch 59
   Lower Moose 62
   Bottom Moose 65
   North Branch 68
      Big Moose Lake 68
   South Branch 72

SACANDAGA RIVER 76
    Sacandaga Lake, Lake Pleasant 76
    Speculator to Northville................................ 78
    Great Sacandaga Lake 82
    East Branch.. 87
    West Branch 90
        Piseco Lake 93
        Lower West Branch 94
        Fall Stream and Vly Lake 96
        Piseco Lake Outlet and Spy Lake....................... 97
SALMON RIVER 99
    Salmon River Reservoir 106
SCHROON RIVER 107
    Schroon Lake 110
WEST CANADA CREEK 116

Canoe Racing...133
Organizations..134
Bibliography 135
Index 136

Adirondack and Tug Hill Rivers

PREFACE

Canoeing can be one of the most calming and peaceful recreational sports. It can be exciting and exhilarating. It can also be very dangerous. In between the desperation and elation of writing this book, I often asked myself, "Why am I doing this?" The answer each time was the same. Safety. If I can make just one person sufficiently aware of the hazards, as well as the joys, of canoeing to prevent a disaster, it will have been worthwhile. I urge you to study the safety code of the American Whitewater Affiliation at the beginning of this book. Learn the river hazards and how to avoid them. I would bet ten to one every time on the skilled, knowledgeable canoeist going over an eighteen-foot waterfall safely against an inexperienced, unaware canoer going down a little stream in high water early in the spring.

Never canoe beyond your ability. Knowledge is a powerful tool. Know ahead what might happen, and know if you can handle any situation. It makes good sense to travel with an experienced paddler (one who has been there before) when going on a new river where there is any possible danger. Don't hesitate to land and study the river from shore when you can't see or don't know what is ahead. Always be respectful of private property.

All things considered, the most dangerous rivers covered in this book are the Boreas, Hudson River Gorge, Lower and Bottom Moose, Upper East Branch of Fish Creek, parts of the Sacandaga, East Canada Creek and Upper West Canada Creek. Approach them with caution, and treat them with respect.

General directions. When descending rivers, right and left banks are always on the right or left when you are heading downstream or toward the sea. Remember that in navigation the three short words go together — *left, port* and *red* (on buoys, etc.), and the three longer words go together — *right, starboard* and *green.*

Clothing. Dress extra warmly in cold weather. It is usually colder on the river than inland due to winds and water openness. On white water it is advisable to wear wetsuits; they could save you from hypothermia. In lieu of a wetsuit wear wool. It keeps you warmer in the water than other materials. Take extra clothing in a waterproof bag made from two garbage bags secured with rubber bands, one up and one down, and put in a duffel bag for protection. The duffel bag is then fastened into your boat for emergency use.

Maps. The USGS maps are made in 15 min. quadrangles, scale 1/62,500, and 7.5 min. quadrangles, scale 1/24,000. The central Adirondack maps are still 15 min. quadrangles, but around the fringes you can now only get the 7.5 min. quadrangles.

When interpreting the maps in this book, be sure you check the scale of the map. Where no scale is indicated, it is the 1/62,500, or approximately one inch to the mile. On the river maps **A** denotes access. It could also be a point of egress. The **E** stands for egress, and means just that. You should not canoe beyond an egress.

In recent years the New York State Department of Transportation (DOT) has been using highway markers when reporting the location of accidents. These markers are placed at .1-mile intervals along each State highway. The top number is the number of the highway; the second designates the region and the county of location. The bottom line indicates the distance north or west from a county or city line. Disregard the first number to obtain the mileage. It is this bottom group of numbers that I have used as the State marker number throughout the book.

Gauge Readings. I look forward to a day in the future when you can call a number and get a gauge reading on a certain river and be assured of good canoeing on that river for that day and for some time following. For now we must be content with help from individuals along the rivers willing to pass along whatever information is available.

Drinking Water. A word of caution about drinking water fresh from a river: Less than two decades ago Stuart Udall and Robert Kennedy, in North Creek for the White Water Derby, quipped before a large audience about drinking the wonderful water from the Hudson River. Today most Adirondack rivers contain *Giardia lamblia*, the causative parasite of *Giardiasis,* sometimes called "beaver fever." It is not to be treated lightly. A friend of mine contracted *Giardiasis* several years ago when we canoed the Missinaibi River to James Bay. He was terribly distressed for two months.

Because the usual water treatments like chlorination do not control it, the New York State Department of Health recommends boiling drinking water for at least three to four minutes or putting it through a DE filter capable of filtering out the cyst, which is ten to twenty microns in size. Globaline is also effective in preventing *Giardiasis.* It would be well to check with your doctor before setting off on a trip for any new developments.

Changes and Corrections. While diligently striving for accuracy in this book, errors and omissions do sneak in or out. Rivers are forever changing, so the author and the Adirondack Mountain Club do not assume responsibility for inaccuracies nor can either be responsible for the safety of people on the rivers.

If you run across any errors, please report them to the Adirondack Mountain Club, 172 Ridge St., Glens Falls, New York 12801.

Acknowledgments.

Many people besides myself are responsible for this book. Other canoers, other writers, friends and associates all made valuable contributions to it. I will mention a few: Margaret Miller, my writing mentor, who helped with history, first drafts and other details, and who managed to slaughter many of my "sacred cows"; Anne Rose Knight, who provided the original art and layout for the maps, and Geralyn Guidetti, who did the final drawings; Carmen Elliott, Neil Woodworth, and Roger Reinicker of the Adirondack Mountain Club who made many helpful suggestions about content; Ed Bielejec of the Mountain Sport Shop at Frankfort, who gave me much information on rivers in the western half of the area covered by the guide; Patrick Cunningham of the Hudson River Rafting Company, who provided helpful details on the Hudson and Sacandaga Rivers; and John Berry, canoeing champion and owner of Millbrook Boats, who gave me much information on rivers in the eastern part of the area.

Friends who accompanied me on the rivers include Hugh Travis, Edward Scotcher, Thomas Gell, Richard Gell, David Blanpied, Connie Thomas, Val Gyrisco, Olga Vrana and Richard Tucker.

I am grateful to Stan Zdunek, boat maker of the Apple Line in Amsterdam, New York, for information and help on canoes.

I would like to thank Alan Brown of the U.S. Geological Survey in Ithaca, New York, for help on maps and flow charts; Marian Holmes of Old Forge for history of that area; and Dwight Webster, Professor Emeritus, Natural Resources, Cornell University, for historical background on the salmon fisheries.

Most of all I am thankful for my mother, Josephine Holley Proskine, who first made me aware of the natural beauty all around us in God's great outdoors. After all these years, it is still to me one of the most rewarding things life has to offer.

September 1984

SAFETY CODE OF THE AMERICAN WHITEWATER AFFILIATION

I. PERSONAL PREPAREDNESS AND RESPONSIBILITY

1. *Be a Competent Swimmer* with ability to handle yourself underwater.

2. *Wear a Lifejacket.*

3. *Keep Your Craft Under Control.* Control must be good enough at all times to stop or reach shore before you reach any danger. Do not enter a rapid unless you are reasonably sure you can safely navigate it or swim the entire rapid in event of capsize.

4. *Be Aware of River Hazards and Avoid Them.* Following are the most frequent *Killers:*

   A. HIGH WATER. The river's power and danger and the difficulty of rescue increase tremendously as the flow rate increases. It is often misleading to judge river level at the put-in. Look at a narrow, critical passage. Could a sudden rise from sun on a snow pack, rain, or a dam release occur on your trip?

   B. COLD. Cold quickly robs one's strength, along with one's will and ability to save oneself. Dress to protect yourself from cold water and weather extremes. When the water temperature is less than 50 degrees F., a diver's wetsuit is essential for safety in event of an upset. Next best is wool clothing under a windproof outer garment such as a splash-proof nylon shell; in this case one should also carry matches and a complete change of clothes in a waterproof package. If, after prolonged exposure, a person experiences uncontrollable shaking or has difficulty talking and moving, he must be warmed immediately by whatever means available.

   C. STRAINERS: Brush, fallen trees, bridge pilings, or anything else which allows river current to sweep through but pins boat and boater against the obstacle. The water pressure on anything trapped this way is overwhelming, and there may be little or no whitewater to warn of danger.

   D. WEIRS, REVERSALS, AND SOUSE HOLES. The water drops over an obstacle, then curls back on itself in a stationary wave, as is often seen at weirs and dams. The surface water is actually going UPSTREAM, and this action will trap any floating object between the drop and the wave. Once trapped, a swimmer's only hope is to dive below the surface where current is flowing downstream, or try to swim out the end of the wave.

5. *Boating Alone* is not recommended. The preferred minimum is three craft.

6. *Have a Frank Knowledge of Your Boating Ability.* Don't attempt waters beyond this ability. Learn paddling skills and teamwork, if in a multiple-manned craft, to match the river you plan to boat.

7. *Be in Good Physical Condition* consistent with the difficulties that may be expected.

8. *Be Practiced in Escape* from an overturned craft, in self rescue, in rescue, and in artificial respiration. Know first aid.

9. *The Eskimo Roll* should be mastered by kayakers and canoers planning to run large rivers and/or rivers with continuous rapids where a swimmer would have trouble reaching shore.

10. *Wear a Crash Helmet* where an upset is likely. This is essential in a kayak or covered canoe.

11. *Be Suitably Equipped.* Wear shoes that will protect your feet during a bad swim or a walk for help, yet will not interfere with swimming (tennis shoes recommended). Carry a knife and waterproof matches. If you need eyeglasses, tie them on and carry a spare pair. Do not wear bulky clothing that will interfere with your swimming when water-logged.

II. BOAT AND EQUIPMENT PREPAREDNESS

1. *Test New and Unfamiliar Equipment* before relying on it for difficult runs.

2. *Be Sure Craft is in Good Repair* before starting a trip. Eliminate sharp projections that could cause injury during a swim.

3. Inflatable craft should have *Multiple Air Chambers* and should be test-inflated before starting a trip.

4. *Have Strong, Adequately Sized Paddles or Oars* for controlling the craft and carry sufficient spares for the length of the trip.

5. *Install Flotation Devices* in non-inflatable craft, securely fixed, and designed to displace as much water from the craft as possible.

6. *Be Certain There is Absolutely Nothing to Cause Entanglement* when coming free from an upset craft; i. e., a spray skirt that won't release or tangles around legs; life jacket buckles, or clothing that might snag; canoe seats that lock on shoe heels; foot

braces that fail or allow feet to jam under them; flexible decks that collapse on boater's legs when a kayak is trapped by water pressure; baggage that dangles in an upset; loose rope in the craft, or badly secured bow/stern lines.

7. *Provide Ropes to Allow You to Hold Onto Your Craft* in case of upset, and so that it may be rescued. Following are the recommended methods:

   A. KAYAKS AND COVERED CANOES should have 6 inch diameter grab loops of ¼ inch rope attached to bow and stern. A stern painter 7 or 8 feet long is optional and may be used if properly secured to prevent entanglement.

   B. OPEN CANOES should have bow and stern lines (painters) securely attached consisting of 8 to 10 feet of ¼ or ⅜ inch rope. These lines must be secured in such a way that they will not come loose accidentally and entangle the boaters during a swim, yet they must be ready for immediate use during an emergency. Attached balls, floats, and knots are *not* recommended.

   C. RAFTS AND DORIES should have taut perimeter grab lines threaded through the loops usually provided.

8. *Respect Rules for Craft Capacity* and know how these capacities should be reduced for whitewater use. (Life raft ratings must generally be halved.)

9. *Carry Appropriate Repair Materials:* tape (heating duct tape) for short trips, complete repair kit for wilderness trips.

10. *Car Top Racks Must Be Strong* and positively attached to the vehicle, and each boat must be tied to each rack. In addition, each end of each boat should be tied to car bumper. Suction cup racks are poor. The entire arrangement should be able to withstand all but the most violent vehicle accident.

III. LEADER'S PREPAREDNESS AND RESPONSIBILITY

   1. *River Conditions.* Have a reasonable knowledge of the difficult parts of the run, or if an exploratory trip, examine maps to estimate the feasibility of the run. Be aware of possible rapid changes in river level, and how these changes can affect the difficulty of the run. If important, determine approximate flow rate or level. If trip involves important tidal currents, secure tide information.

   2. *Participants.* Inform participants of expected river conditions and determine if the prospective boaters are qualified for the trip. All decisions should be based on group safety and comfort. Difficult decisions on the participation of marginal

boaters must be based on total group strength.

3. *Equipment.* Plan so that all necessary group equipment is present on the trip; 50 to 100 foot throwing rope, first aid kit with fresh and adequate supplies, extra paddles, repair materials, and survival equipment if appropriate. Check equipment as necessary at the put-in, especially life jackets, boat flotation, and any items that could prevent complete escape from the boat in case of an upset.

4. *Organization.* Remind each member of individual responsibility in keeping group compact and intact between leader and sweep (capable rear boater). If group is too large, divide into smaller groups, each of appropriate boating strength, and designate leaders and sweeps.

5. *Float Plan.* If trip is into a wilderness area, or for an extended period, your plans should be filed with appropriate authorities, or left with someone who will contact them after a certain time. Establishment of checkpoints along the way at which civilization could be contacted if necessary should be considered. Knowing location of possible help could speed rescue in any case.

IV. IN CASE OF UPSET

1. *Evacuate Your Boat Immediately* if there is imminent danger of being trapped against logs, brush, or any other form of strainer.

2. *Recover With an Eskimo Roll if Possible.*

3. *If You Swim, Hold onto Your Craft.* It has much flotation and is easy for rescuers to spot. Get to the upstream end so craft cannot crush you against obstacles.

4. *Release Your Craft if This Improves Your Safety.* If rescue is not imminent and water is numbing cold, or if worse rapids follow, then strike out for the nearest shore.

5. *When Swimming Rocky Rapids, Use Backstroke with Legs Downstream and Feet Near the Surface.* If your foot wedges on the bottom, fast water will push you under and hold you there. Get to Slow or Very Shallow Water before Trying to Stand or Walk. Look Ahead. Avoid possible entrapment situations: rock wedges, fissures, strainers, brush, logs, weirs, reversals and souse holes. Watch for eddies and slack water so that you can be ready to use these when you approach. Use every opportunity to work your way toward shore.

6. If others spill, *Go After the Boaters.* Rescue boats and equipment only if this can be done safely.

A New System of Universal River Signals

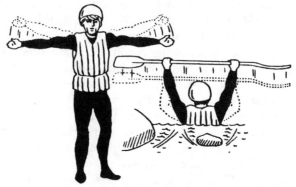

STOP: Potential hazard ahead. Wait for "all clear" signal before proceeding, or scout ahead. Form a horizontal bar with your paddle or outstretched arms. Move up and down to attract attention, using a pumping motion with paddle or flying motion with arms. Those seeing the signal should pass it back to others in the party.

HELP/EMERGENCY: Assist the signaler as quickly as possible. Give three long blasts on a police whistle while waving a paddle, helmet or life vest over your head in a circular motion. If a whistle is not available, use the visual signal alone. A whistle is best carried on a lanyard attached to the shoulder of a life vest.

ALL CLEAR: Come ahead (In the absence of other directions, proceed down the center). Form a vertical bar with your paddle or one arm held high above your head. Paddle blade should be turned flat for maximum visibility. To signal direction or a preferred course through a rapid around obstruction, lower the previously vertical "all clear" by 45 degrees toward the side of the river with the preferred route. Never point toward the obstacle you wish to avoid.

Signaling system devised by AWA committee composed of Jim Sindelar, Tom McCloud, O.K. Goodwin, Bev Hartline, Walt Blackadar and Charles Walbridge. Illustrations by Les Fry.

INTERNATIONAL SCALE OF RIVER DIFFICULTY

(If rapids on a river generally fit into one of the following classifications, but the water temperature is below 50 degrees F., or if the trip is an extended one in a wilderness area, the river should be considered one class more difficult than normal.)

CLASS I. Moving water with a few riffles and small waves. Few or no obstructions.

CLASS II. Easy rapids with waves up to three feet and wide, clear channels that are obvious without scouting. Some maneuvering is required.

CLASS III. Rapids with high, irregular waves often capable of swamping an open canoe. Narrow passages that often require complex maneuvering. May require scouting from shore.

CLASS IV. Long, difficult rapids with constricted passages that often require precise maneuvering in very turbulent waters. Scouting from shore is often necessary, and conditions make rescue difficult. Generally not possible for open canoes. Boaters in covered canoes and kayaks should be able to Eskimo roll.

CLASS V. Extremely difficult, long, and very violent rapids with highly congested routes which nearly always must be scouted from shore. Rescue conditions are difficult and there is a significant hazard to life in event of a mishap. Ability to Eskimo roll is essential for kayaks and canoes.

CLASS VI. Difficulties of Class V carried to the extreme of navigability. Nearly impossible and very dangerous. For teams of experts only, after close study and with all precautions taken.

FLOW CHART OF RIVERS

The following rivers have records of flow made by the U.S. Geological Survey for the past thirty-five years. The suggested optimum gauge readings are estimates from local canoeists.

River	Discharge (CFS) Max.	Min.	Cu. Ft./Sec. Average	Gauge (ft.) Max.	Min.	Suggested optimum for canoeing (ft.)
East Canada Creek	24,000	.05	681	9.0	.47	3-5
Fish Creek	14,500	30	543	11.71	.44	2.5-5
Hudson (North Creek)	28,900	112	1,059	12.14	1.96	4-6
Indian	3,460	1	296	7.8	.00	3-5
Moose	18,700	107	807	17.45	1.64	2-4
Sacandaga (near Hope)	32,000	16	1,102	11.0	1.17	3-5
Schroon	12,100	76	784	12.18	.80	2-3.5
West Canada Creek	23,300	20	1,318	10.47	.90	2-5

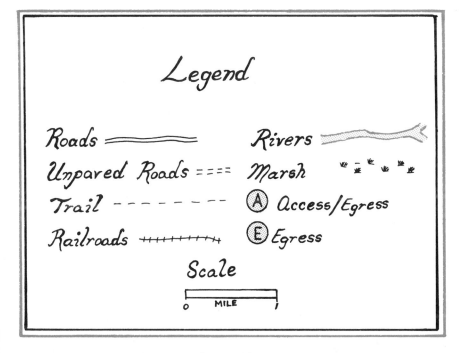

Legend

Roads ═══════ Rivers

Unpaved Roads ════ Marsh

Trail ──────── (A) Access/Egress

Railroads ++++++++ (E) Egress

Scale

0   MILE   1

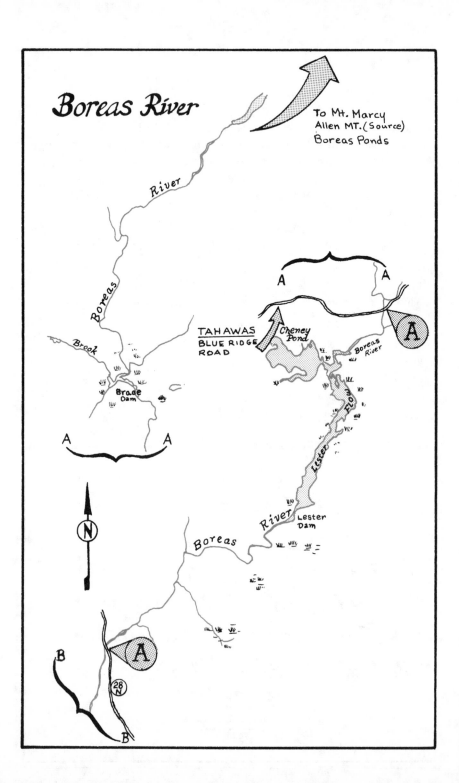

BOREAS RIVER

Boreas River

Tributary: Hudson River

County: Essex

U.S.G.S. Maps: 15-minute 1/62500
Newcomb, Schroon Lake, Mt. Marcy

Total Length: 24 mi.

Cruising Length: 14.5 mi.

Season Recommended: April-Mid-May

Campsites: Harris Lake Public Campsite
Eagle Point Public Campsite

Access	Location	Elev. Feet	Distance Miles	Inter. Dist.	Drop Feet	Gradient Ft./Mile	Rating Class
	Source: Allen Mountain White Lily Brook	3,400	24		2,280	95	
	Boreas Pond	1,973	21				
A	Blue Ridge Tahawus Rd. Bridge	1,728	14.5	6.5	124	19	III
A	NY 28N Bridge	1,594	8	6.5	368	56	V
A	Northwoods Club Road Bridge	1,226	1.5	1.5	86	57	III
	Jct. Hudson River	1,140	0				

The wild Boreas River flows out of the northern, or Boreal, forest, just as its name implies. It rises on the south slope of Allen Mountain, which is three miles south of Mt. Marcy, and is one-half mile west of the stream that feeds Upper Ausable Lake. Only expert kayakers should attempt the Boreas. This river is a solid Class IV-V at Medium-High levels and is not a trip for an open canoe.

The Boreas River must be high to be canoed. About the only check on this is the gauge on the Hudson at North Creek (call 518-251-3215). If the Hudson is running at six feet or more, the Boreas probably will be runnable. Since the two watersheds are some distance apart, however, they may get different amounts of rainfall, so the reading at North Creek is not an absolute guarantee of the level on the Boreas. If the Boreas is at flood stage (over 6½ ft.) it is too dangerous to run.

It is possible to launch your boat at the bridge on the Blue Ridge-Tahawus Road (Cty. Road 2B), which is about six miles east of the NY 28N junction. Below the bridge is Lester Flow, all flat water for about two miles. Most of the 124-foot drop in the six and four-tenths-mile stretch between Blue Ridge-Tahawus and 28N comes below the Flow.

A second launching spot is above the NY 28N bridge. There is parking and access on the left bank. To look over this section of the river, you can follow a trail which goes along the left bank of the river for about a mile down to Hewitt Eddy and then goes west to 28N. (It was along this road that Theodore Roosevelt became the twenty-sixth President of the United States on receiving word of the unexpected death of President McKinley.) You first come to Hewitt Eddy, which is stillwater, and below that Vanderwhacker Brook comes in on the right. From here on down to the Hudson, the Delaware and Hudson Railroad bed is on the right bank.

The stream from Vanderwhacker junction drops only about thirty-six feet in the next two and six-tenths miles. Then, at approximately 2½ miles, the world suddenly tips, and your boat starts flying by trees, boulders and water so fast you think you are in a new world of water. It becomes sheer ecstasy, or terror, depending on your ability and the water conditions. In the next two and two-tenths miles the river drops two hundred and fifty-four feet, with a gradient of one hundred eleven feet per mile, making it the steepest canoeable river in the Adirondacks for this distance.

On September 15, 1984, William Lynch, Peter Hornbeck and I visited the Boreas. We checked the gradient of the river in three places by actual measurement and found a seven-foot drop in eighty feet horizontally, an eight-foot drop in 100 feet and a five-foot drop in thirty feet. If extended, these would be gradients of 482 feet, 422 feet and 874 feet per mile. Fortunately, the river does not continue with such drops, but this does give one some idea of the steep stretches in the river. Be sure to scout this section. It can be dangerous.

At the Northwoods Club Road bridge is another good access. Here there are several campsites suitable for tents and a couple that are

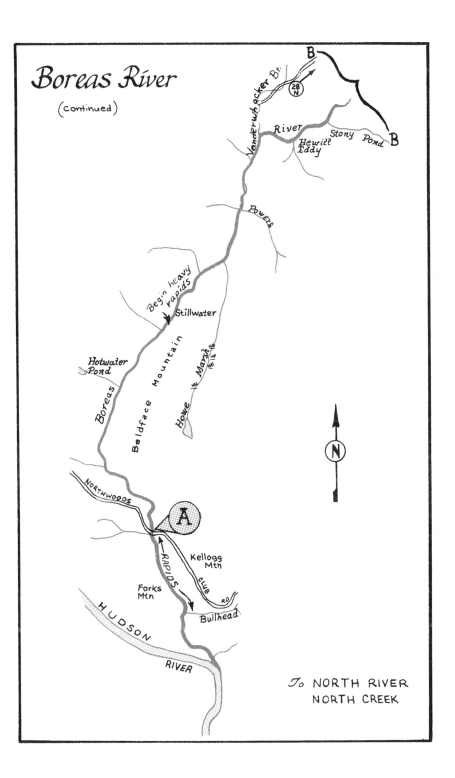

Boreas River

(continued)

Vanderwhacker Br.

28
N

B

River

Hewitt
Eddy

Stony Pond

B

Powers

Begin heavy rapids

Stillwater

Hotwater
Pond

Baldface Mountain

Howe Marsh

Boreas

N

NORTHWOODS

A

Kellogg
Mtn

RAPIDS

CLUB

Forks
Mtn

RD.

Bullhead

HUDSON

RIVER

To NORTH RIVER
NORTH CREEK

suitable for small trailers. Pit toilets are provided both above and below the bridge. Below the bridge the river moderates and falls eighty-six feet in the mile and a half to the Hudson, or fifty-seven feet per mile. When you reach the Hudson, the best way out is to continue on down the river to North River and take out on the right bank at the Warren County "Canoe Access" sign.

An excellent article by Clyde Smith entitled "Heavy Water" appeared in the May/June 1981 issue of *Adirondack Life*. When asked, "What would you consider the most horrendous canoeable river in the Adirondacks?" Clyde answered, "Taking into consideration all the optimum conditions — high water, steep gradient, narrow width, and remoteness — my choice would be the Boreas."

CEDAR RIVER

Cedar River

Tributary: Hudson River

Counties: Hamilton, Essex

U.S.G.S. Maps: 15-minute 1/62500
Newcomb, Blue Mountain, Indian Lake, West Canada Lakes

Total Length: 37 mi.

Cruising Length: River — 13 mi.
Flow — 4 mi.

Season Recommended: Flow-All-season;
River—April-Mid-May

Campsites: Wakely Dam, Moose River
Recreational Area, Lake Durant
Public Campsite

Access	Location	Elev. Feet	Distance Miles	Inter. Dist.	Drop Feet	Gradient Ft./Mile	Rating Class
	Source:						
	Cedar Lakes	2,442	37		1,017	27	
				7	342	50	
	Lean-to Upper						
	Cedar River Flow	2,100	30				
				4	0	0	I
A	Wakely Dam	2,100	26				
	Dangerous: Skip this section			13	438	34	III-VI
A	NY 28 Bridge	1,662	13				
				13	237	18	III
	Jct. Hudson River	1,425	0				

The fabulous Cedar River, its banks lined with northern white cedar, starts out of Cedar Lakes in the West Canada Lakes Wilderness Area in the very center of Hamilton County. It is adjacent to the West Canada drainage system on the south and the Moose River drainage system on the west. It flows northeasterly down through Cedar River Flow, then easterly into the Hudson River.

The Northville-Placid Trail is on the west side of Cedar Lakes and crosses the river just below the outlet. The river drops fast, 342 feet in seven miles, down to the Cedar River Flow. The trail crosses again to the left bank just above the stillwater, then goes by a lean-to on the left bank of the stream. There is room here for additional tents and plenty of firewood, making it a good spot for an overnight stay on Cedar River Flow. There is another nice campsite on a piney knoll on the right (east) bank before the Flow widens.

As you paddle down the channel in late summer you will see meadowsweet, spirea, common elderberry and swampcandles (yellow loosestrife) in bloom. You can usually hear a loon calling in its haunting tremulo. After one mile of channel the Flow opens wider and it is three miles to Wakely Dam, which backs up water in the Flow. (The dam was originally built to flush logs and pulp down the Cedar River to the mills below. My friend George Osgood remembers watching, as a young boy of fifteen working as a water boy, the logs charging down the river.) Around the dam there are many campsites maintained by the DEC.

The Cedar River Flow is great for a late summer or fall canoe-camping trip. It can, of course, be done earlier in the season, but the black flies and mosquitos will be there, too, and in sufficient numbers to do battle.

To reach the Flow, turn southwest off NY 28 about two miles west of the junction of NY 30 and NY 28 in Indian Lake Village at the sign for the Moose River Recreation Area. Follow the Cedar River Road (CR 12) for eleven miles up to the Wakely Dam (foot of Cedar River Flow) where the Cedar River entrance to the Moose River Recreational Area is located.

For an interesting drive through the Moose River plains, start at the Cedar River entrance. It is about forty miles through to the eastern gate at Limekiln Public Campsite, which is near the village of Inlet on NY 28.

Below Wakely Dam, the river drops 328 feet in the seven miles down to the Sprague Brook junction, and there is a rocky chasm with vertical drops near the town line about two miles below the dam. From my observations, this is an impassable section of the stream. The river is very narrow, and the chances of debris and strainers are likely. It's best to skip the entire section.

A good starting place on the Cedar River is at the NY 28 bridge. On

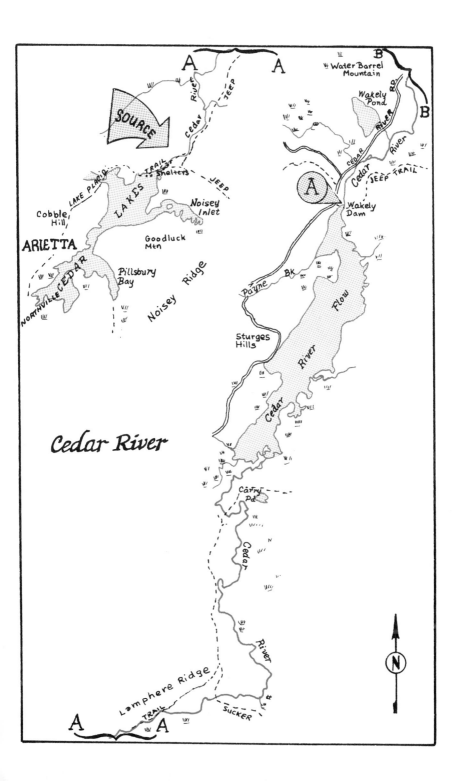

Cedar River

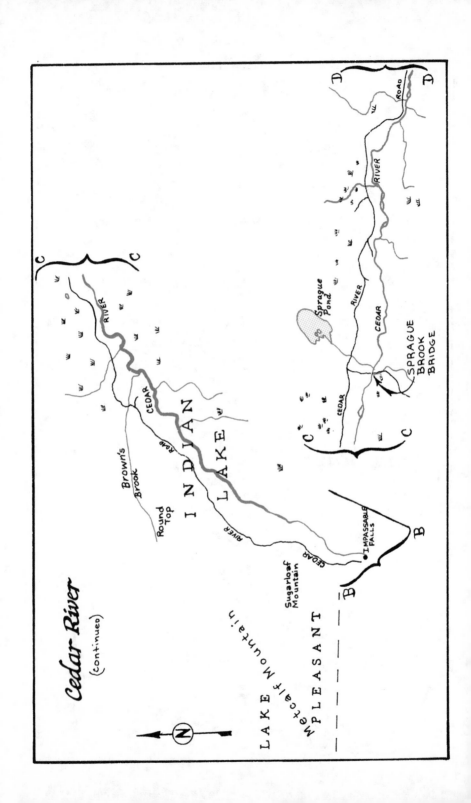

Cedar River
(continued)

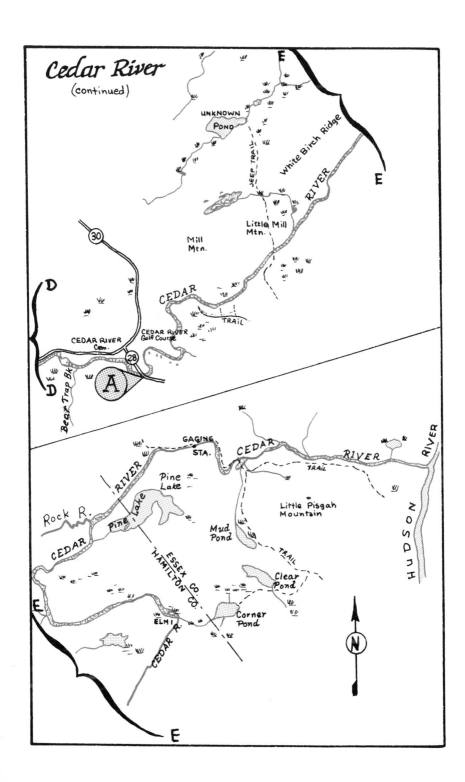

the right bank just below the bridge is the boat shop of John B. Spring. He repairs Adirondack guideboats and wooden canoes. John thinks the Cedar is a "fabulous" river, and he likes to talk about it and his craft.

The river drops 237 feet in its thirteen-mile descent to the Hudson. There are Class III rapids before the junction of Rock River. The outlet of the Essex Chain of Lakes flows into Rock River above the junction. Just below the Rock River junction, which is on the left, Pine Lake Outlet comes in on the right. Pine Lake is mostly on State land and provides an excellent place to camp. Three-pound brook trout have been taken from Pine Lake.

Stillwater follows below Pine Lake Outlet for several miles. The last quarter mile before the Cedar joins the Hudson has a steep rocky chute with a total drop of about ten feet.

When the Cedar is running high, it makes quite a surge where it flows into the Hudson. On the right bank at the junction is another good camping spot.

The only way out from the foot of the Cedar is by way of the Hudson River. Take the three-mile stretch down (south) to the junction of the Indian, where there is a trail on the right bank between the two rivers leading up to the road and out to Indian Lake Village (NY 28).

EAST CANADA CREEK

East Canada Creek

Tributary: Mohawk River

Counties: Hamilton, Fulton, Montgomery, Herkimer

U.S.G.S. Maps: 7.5-minute 1/24000
Stratford, Little Falls, Oppenheim, Fort Plains
15-minute 1/62500
Piseco Lake

Total Length: 35 mi.

Cruising Length: 17 mi.

Season Recommended: April—Mid-May

Campsites: Caroga Lake Public Campsite
Informal: Powley Rd. (State land)

Access	Location	Elev. Feet	Distance Miles	Inter. Dist.	Drop Feet	Gradient Ft./Mile	Rating Class
	Source:						
	Morehouse Lake	1,975	34.8		1,657	47	
	Christian Lake	1,950	32.3				
A	Powley Place	1,665	29.3				I
				4.2	215	51	IV
A	Bridge below Oregon	1,450	25.1				
				7.1	382	54	IV
A	Stratford (NY 29 Bridge)	1,068	18				
				3	181	60	IV
A	Emmonsburg Bridge	887	15				
				6.6	99	15	III
E	Dolgerville Bridge	788	8.4				
				3.9	262	67	Improbable
	Ingraham Mills Bridge	526	4.5				
				4.5	208	46	Improbable
	Jct. Mohawk River	318	0		Bottom Half Mile		III

Tempestuous East Canada Creek, so named by early settlers because it came from the direction of Canada, flows out of Christian Lake, which is northeast of Big Goldmine Hill and four miles southwest of Irondequoit Bay in Piseco Lake. The area is characterized by unexpected names like Jockeybush Lake, Blind Man's Vly, Punkhole, and Tomany Mountain.

To get into the upper East Canada Creek region, take NY 10 south from its junction with NY 8, eight miles west of the village of Lake Pleasant and just south of Higgins Bay on Piseco Lake. After crossing the bridge over the outlet of Piseco Lake, turn right at State Marker No. 1133 onto Powley Road, a delightful back country road through the southern Adirondacks which comes out at Stratford. There are many informal campsites along this road where you can pitch a tent or pull in with a small camp trailer.

Eight and two-tenths miles from NY 10 you come to Powley Place where the road crosses East Canada Creek. Powley Place is one of those spots you wish could talk and tell you its past history. Today it is only a sign by the bridge under which languidly flows East Canada Creek. The cleared, sandy land suggests that there may have been a farm here, or perhaps a sawmill or a logging camp. A low beaver dam keeps the water above the bridge passable for about one-half mile. For about two miles the trip down the stream is easy and interesting, stillwater with an 18-inch beaver dam to cross. In late June you see American mountain ash and wild raisin in bloom; on the north bank pink azalea (pinkster) and mountain laurel.

As the creek approaches the road, you hear whitewater ahead. This is the start of one of the wilder canoe trips in the Adirondacks. From this point down to Stratford it is a steep and mostly continuous rock garden.

Other starting places are at Stratford or at the bridge below Oregon, which is 6.5 miles north of Stratford. The 7.1-mile stretch into Stratford is a really wild whitewater trip. At high water it is a Class III-plus to Class IV water, depending on the flow. The stream is about 50 to 75 feet wide, narrowing down to 20 feet in the rock-ribbed chasm about two miles above Stratford. Scout the stream bed to be sure there are no strainers. It is best to do this section with someone who has been through it before. It drops at the rate of over 50 feet per mile.

At Stratford there is access at the NY 29 bridge. From this point to Emmonsburg is a three-mile, sixty-foot-per-mile boulder patch, which requires scouting. Some ledges may necessitate a short carry depending on water levels.

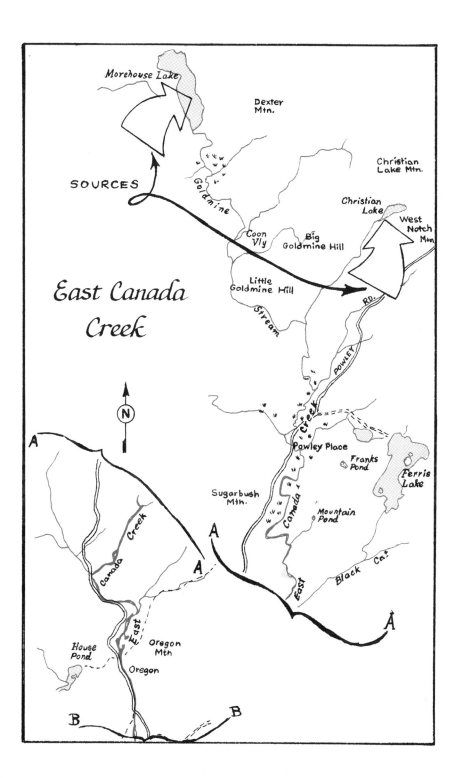

East Canada Creek

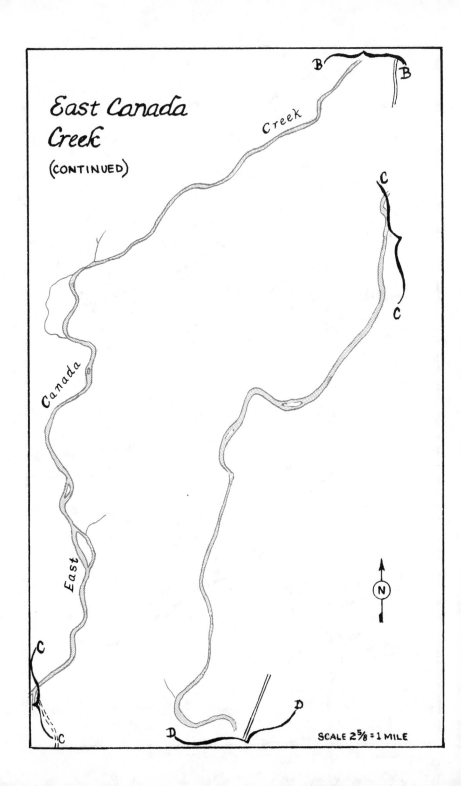

East Canada
Creek
(CONTINUED)

Creek

Canada

East

B

B

C

C

C

C

D

D

N

SCALE 2⅝ = 1 MILE

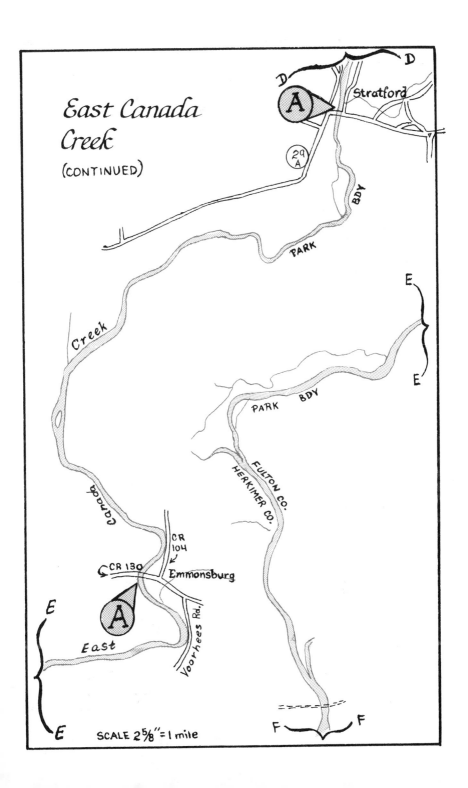

East Canada Creek
(CONTINUED)

D

D

Stratford

A

29
A

PARK

BDY

Creek

E

E

PARK BDY

FULTON CO.

HERKIMER CO.

Canada

CR
104

CR 130

Emmonsburg

A

Voorhees Rd.

E

East

E

F

F

SCALE 2⅝" = 1 mile

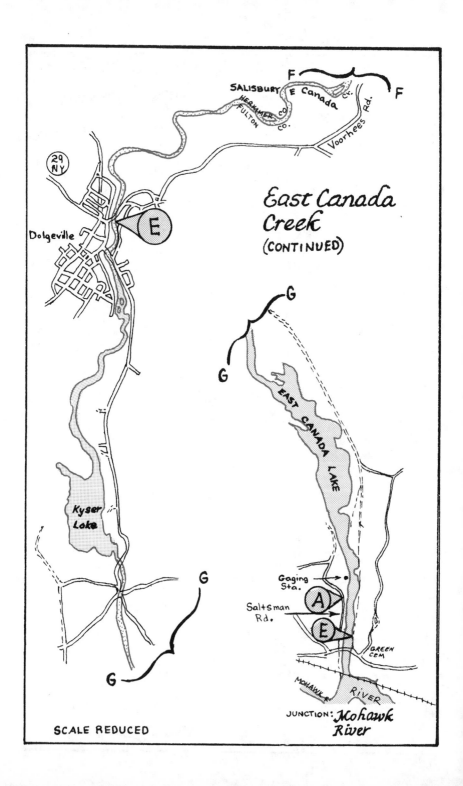

SALISBURY

F

E Canada
Cr.

HERKIMER CO.

FULTON CO.

Voorhees Rd.

F

29
NY

*East Canada
Creek*
(CONTINUED)

Dolgeville

E

G

G

EAST CANADA LAKE

Kyser
Lake

Gaging
Sta.

G

A

Saltsman
Rd.

E

G

GREEN
CEM

MOHAWK R.

RIVER

G

JUNCTION: *Mohawk
River*

SCALE REDUCED

From Emmonsburg to the Dolgeville NY 29 bridge, the river flattens out and averages a drop of 15 feet per mile in the five and six-tenths miles. Take out at the bridge as there are dams and high waterfalls below. There is a whitewater play area in the half-mile above the NY 5 bridge up to the Niagara-Hudson hydroelectric plant. Go up the right bank of the creek (left as you look upstream) on the Stutzman Road and put in where the road bears left away from the river. When water is being released from the East Canada Lake through the power plant some nice Class III rapids are formed. This usually occurs midday, but there is no set schedule and no phone number to call at this time.

The upper river can usually be canoed April through early May and at other times of heavy rainfall over the area.

FISH CREEK

Mysterious Fish Creek is a great fishing stream and one of the most spectacular, though one of the lesser known, streams of the state. From the moment you shove off, especially when the water is high, you feel as though you are on the fabled "River of No Return." Because of the cliffs on either side, there is no egress until you reach Point Rock, Rome Reservoir or Palmer Road Bridge. The many waterfalls caused by the spring freshets coming off the gorge walls give this waterway its mystical character.

A trip down this Class II and III stream is an exhilarating experience. My friend Ed Bielejec, a boatman very familiar with the streams of the eastern Adirondacks and Tug Hill, describes the creek this way: "It is the prettiest river in this part of the world, with eighteen waterfalls coming in on top of you from the various creeks and tumbling into the basin. It is cut into the shale 90 feet deep in some places, and it is very seldom seen by other than boaters."

Fish Creek came by its name ecologically. Back in 1810 Dewitt Clinton, on his inspection of the route of the contemplated Erie Canal, noted in his journal that on July 13th of that year he and his company had supper at Mrs. Jackson's Tavern at the eastern end of Oneida Lake near the mouth of Fish Creek. He wrote:

"Fish Creek enters Wood Creek, a mile from the (Oneida) Lake, on the north side. It is much larger and deeper, and derives its name from the excellent fish with which it abounds, up to the Falls, which are ten miles from its mouth. It is frequented by great numbers of salmon; and we saw Indians with spears after the fish, and met two canoes going on the same business, with their pine knots and apparatus ready for the attack."

Today the salmon are gone, but walleyes run up the creek from Oneida Lake to spawn. The upper section is popular with trout fishermen.

Fish Creek

Tributary: Oneida Lake	**Total Length:** 54 mi. (W. Branch 36 mi.)
Counties: Oneida, Lewis	**Cruising Length:** Fish Creek and E. Branch 37 mi.; W. Branch 21 mi.
U.S.G.S. Maps: 7.5-minute 1/24000 *High Market, Verona Point Rock Lee Center, Camden East, Sylvan Beach*	**Season Recommended:** April-May
	Campsites: Whetstone Gulf Public Campsite Pixley Falls State Park

Access	Location	Elev. Feet	Distance Miles	Inter. Dist.	Drop Feet	Gradient Ft./Mile	Rating Class
12							
	East Branch						
	Source: Swamp West of Whetstone	1,980	54		1,611	30	
	Fish Creek	1,540	37				
				12	565	47	III
A	Bridge near Point Rock	975	25				
				4.2	275	65	III
	Rome Reservoir	700	20.8				
				1.9	100	50	III
A	Palmer Road Bridge	600	18.9				
				1.8	106	54	III
A	Taberg Bridge	494	17.1				
				2.9	95	32	II
	Jct. East and West Branches	399	14.2				
				6.2	21	3	I
A	Herder Bridge NY 49	378	8.0				
				8	9	1	I
A	Oneida Lake	369	0				
	West Branch						
	Source: Maple Hill on Potter Creek	895	36		496	14	
				15	369	25	
A	Westdale Bridge	526	21				
				9	28	3	I
A	Camden Bridge	498	12				
				8	60	8	I-II
A	McConnellsville Bridge	438	4				
				4	39	10	I-II
	Jct. East and West Branches	399	0				

EAST BRANCH

To approach the East Branch of Fish Creek from the south, east or west, get on NY 26 at Rome and go north about twelve miles to West

Branch, then east to the Taberg-Point Rock Road. Proceed north to Point Rock and take the left fork just north of the hamlet until you come to Fish Creek. The access is on the left bank just below the bridge.

Starting from the stillwater and keeping right, close to the cliff, you go down through a fast little chute, through another pool and over a shoals. From this point you are committed to the fast-moving stream through the rocky gorge. Six-tenths of a mile down from the bridge, Point Rock Creek comes in on the left. There is a possible exit from the river here, taking out on the left bank at the junction and following a trail up the steep hill. You will come to an open field which is only two-tenths of a mile from the Point Rock Road.

The next possible exit from the river is the Rome Reservoir, which is about three miles down the river from the bridge mentioned above. This reservoir, which is only about 500 feet long, has high rocky banks and a dam about 20 feet high. If you keep to the left bank, you will find a landing site about 50 feet above the dam. There is a ramp down to the water's edge. To get out you must climb a steep road up from the left bank about three-tenths of a mile until you come to the padlocked gate at the macadam road. To reach Taberg, take the road to the right. Since the reservoir is posted, use this exit only in an emergency.

From here on to Taberg, the river is fast. The river bends left and then right over a large ledge, forming a keeper. I call it Big Keeper because I cracked a knee here (and lost a sneaker). Beware! The rocky gorge continues to the junction of Fall Creek and then widens somewhat. At the junction of Florence Creek, the area adjacent to the stream widens even more, and the banks are less steep. Below Palmer Road Bridge, the bank on the right soon flattens out entirely.

I stress the topography of the stream as a warning to novices not to attempt going down it in high water. Three canoeists have lost their lives here in recent years. You should have plenty of skill, good equipment, and an experienced team of whitewater boatmen.

Ed Bielejec said of a high water trip on Fish Creek in 1982: "There were no eddies. You tore down through the gorge with no way out." Ed is a leader of white water trips throughout the northeast and a man worth listening to. He runs the Mountain Sports Shop at Frankfurt, New York. You can call him at 315-733-5458 to get information about water depth and running conditions.

After the gorge, the next access is on the left bank just above Palmer Road Bridge. The next egress is on the right bank under the second bridge in the hamlet of Taberg. About one mile below this bridge, the river flattens out, with Class I water down to Herder (NY 49) Bridge, where there is another access.

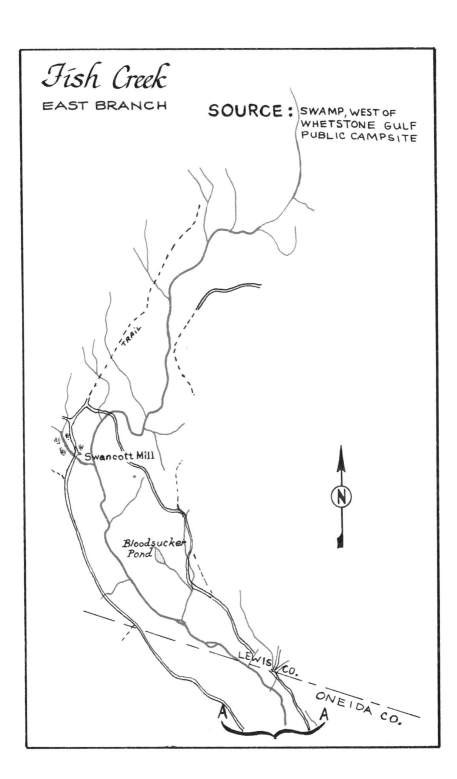

Fish Creek
EAST BRANCH

SOURCE: SWAMP, WEST OF WHETSTONE GULF PUBLIC CAMPSITE

TRAIL

Swancott Mill

Bloodsucker Pond

N

LEWIS CO.

ONEIDA CO.

A   A

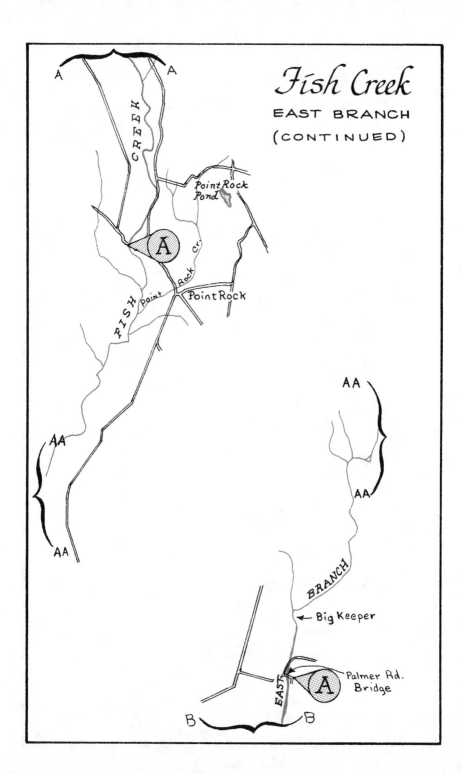

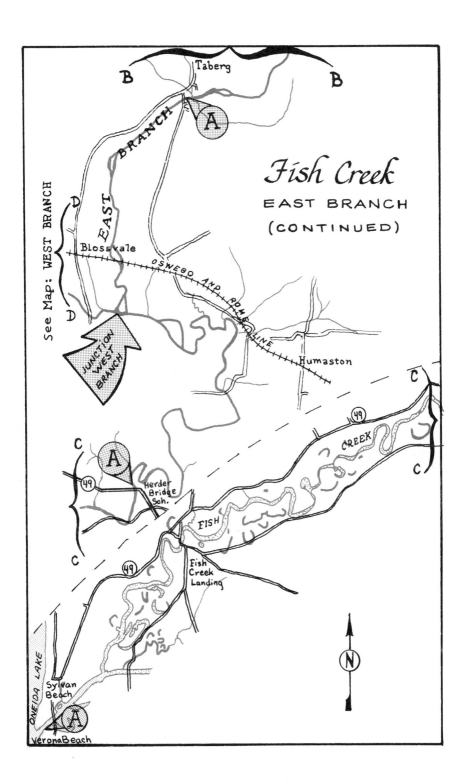

Taberg

B   B

EAST BRANCH

A

Fish Creek

EAST BRANCH

(CONTINUED)

D

See Map: WEST BRANCH

Blossvale

OSWEGO AND ROME LINE

D

JUNCTION WEST BRANCH

Humaston

C   C

C   C

CREEK

49

A

C

49

Herder Bridge Sch.

FISH

Fish Creek Landing

49

ONEIDA LAKE

Sylvan Beach

A

Verona Beach

N

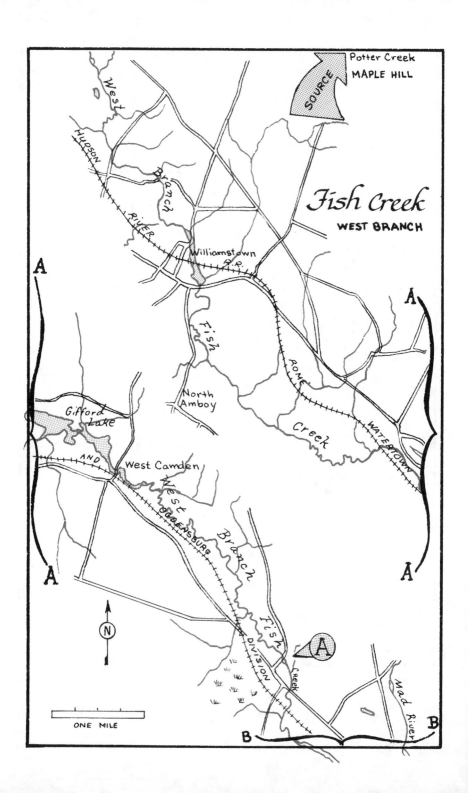

Potter Creek
MAPLE HILL

SOURCE

Fish Creek
WEST BRANCH

West

Hudson

Branch

River

Williamstown R.R.

A

A

Fish

Rome

North
Amboy

Creek

WATERTOWN

Gifford
Lake

AND

West Camden

West

OGDENSBURG

Branch

Fish

A

A

A

DIVISION

Fish

Creek

A

Mad River

N

B

B

ONE MILE

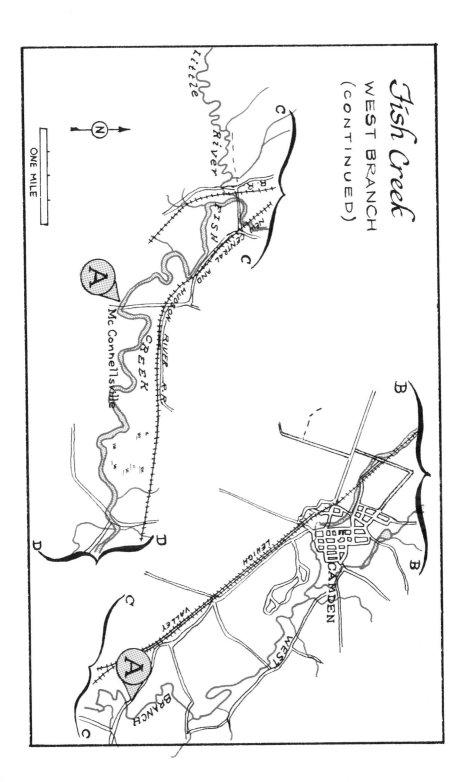

Fish Creek
WEST BRANCH
(CONTINUED)

ONE MILE

N

Little Fish River

FISH

B

C

NEW YORK CENTRAL AND HUDSON RIVER R.R.

C

C

A

McConnellsville

CREEK

D

D

B

B

CAMDEN

LEHIGH

WEST

VALLEY

BRANCH

C

C

A

The West Branch of Fish Creek comes in on the right two and nine-tenths miles below Taberg. From Herder Bridge to Sylvan Beach the river drops only nine feet. It twists and turns through a swampy area and is full of oxbows. You may take out in Sylvan Beach just above the main street or on Oneida Lake at the New York State boat launching site just west of NY 13 on the southeast corner of the lake.

You will need to be cautious of Oneida Lake. Strong winds can come up without warning and can make very high and choppy waves. If the water is four feet or above on the gauge at Taberg lower bridge, it is possible to start about thirteen miles upstream from Point Rock Bridge. Go to the hamlet of Fish Creek on Lewis County Route 47 and put in on the Kotery Road or on Alder Creek. To locate access points, it is easier if you go with someone who has traveled the river before. You might want to check with Ed Bielejec of Mountain Sports for scheduled trips.

WEST BRANCH

The West Branch of Fish Creek is a delightful stream flowing through a pastoral setting of forest and farms. In the spring, at medium high or high water, it is a lively stream with plenty of small rapids and pools. Lawrence Grinnell describes the West Branch in *Canoeable Waterways of New York State and Vicinity* as "one of the finest canoeable runs in the Central New York Region. Emerging from forest near Blossvale the river tore along to a turbulent junction with the East Branch. Here complicated eddies, formed at the convergence of the two branches, on transverse aspects, exhibit noticeably raised elongated mounds of whitewater."

A good day's trip on the West Branch would be from Westdale down to the junction of the east branch—a total of 21 miles. In Camden, you have to portage 100 ft. left at the dam. You also must portage left at the dam in McConnellsville, where the famous Harden Furniture Company is located along the river.

I would take out at the bridge between Blossvale and Pine, about one-eighth mile above the junction with the East Branch of Fish Creek unless you prefer flat water, in which case you may go on down the main stream another six miles and take out on the left bank at the Herder Bridge on NY 49.

HUDSON RIVER

The magnificent Hudson River we are covering here is not the Hudson as most people think of it, a big river of commerce, tides, estuary, Day Lines, the route of the New York Central Railroad, highlands and baronial estates. Rather, it is a beautiful stream that starts high in the Adirondack Mountains of New York State.

When most people talk about the source of the Hudson they mention Lake Tear of the Clouds. This is romantic sounding; however, the Hudson's real source is every drop of rain, every snowflake, that falls on the south and west slopes of Mt. Marcy and all the other drops that fall in the drainage system.

To see the sources, go up the Opalescent River and Feldspar Brook and other trails in the vicinity. You will be rewarded by the vastness and grandeur of the wilderness, the overpowering mountains and the beauty of falling water.

The Hudson, named for Henry Hudson the explorer in 1609, has everything for the canoer and the kayaker: miles of stillwater above Hadley Luzerne, gentle rifts near Warrensburg, rushing waters above The Glen, and the surging turbulence of the gorge.

SANFORD LAKE TO NEWCOMB

To do all of the Hudson you can start at the north end of Sanford Lake, which is about 8 miles northeast of Newcomb. Actually, the river flows out of Henderson Lake two miles upriver from Sanford Lake. Henderson Lake was named for a man who opened an iron mine on the Hudson in the early 1800s. He was later killed accidentally by his own pistol on Calamity Brook. A large sign on the road near the mines gives much information about the industry. Three-mile-long Sanford Lake was narrowed in some places by the tailings from the mine. If you

Hudson River

Tributary: Atlantic Ocean

Counties: Saratoga, Warren, Essex

U.S.G.S. Maps: 15-minute 1/62500
*Mt. Marcy, Newcomb, Santanoni
Thirteenth Lake, North Creek,
Lake Luzerne*

Total Length: 87 mi. above Hadley-Luzerne
(275 mi. above New York City)

Cruising Length: 79 mi.

Season Recommended: April, May, Mid-June
and releases from Indian Lake
(Call 518-251-3215)

Campsites: Lewey Lake Public Campsite
Harris Lake Public Campsite
Luzerne Public Campsite

Access	Location	Elev. Feet	Distance Miles	Inter. Dist.	Drop Feet	Gradient Ft./Mile	Rating Class
	Source:						
	Lake Tear-of-the-Clouds	4,320	87				
	Henderson Lake	1,810	81				
				16	258	16	III
A	Newcomb NY 28 Bridge	1,552	65				
				5	57	11	III
	Jct. Goodnow R.	1,495	60				
				4	24	6	II
	Jct. Cedar R.	1,467	56				
				3	45	15	II
A	Jct. Indian R.	1,422	53				
				8	282	35	V
	Jct. Boreas R.	1,140	45				
				5	88	18	III
A	North River	1,052	40				
				5	64	13	II
A	North Creek	988	35				
				7	120	17	III
A	Riparius	868	28				
				6	146	24	III
A	The Glen	722	22				
				22	157	7	II
E	Take-out above Hadley-Luzerne Falls (188 mi. from NYC)	565	0				

are combining a canoeing-hiking adventure, there are several trailheads in this region leading into the high peaks. The start of the trail to Santanoni, Panther and Couchsachraga (Couchie) is at the north end of Sanford Lake. At the north end of this road are the trails to Indian Pass, The Flowed Lands, Avalanche Pass, Mt. Marcy and others. For detailed trail descriptions, see *Guide to Adirondack Trails—High Peak Region,* published by the Adirondack Mountain Club.

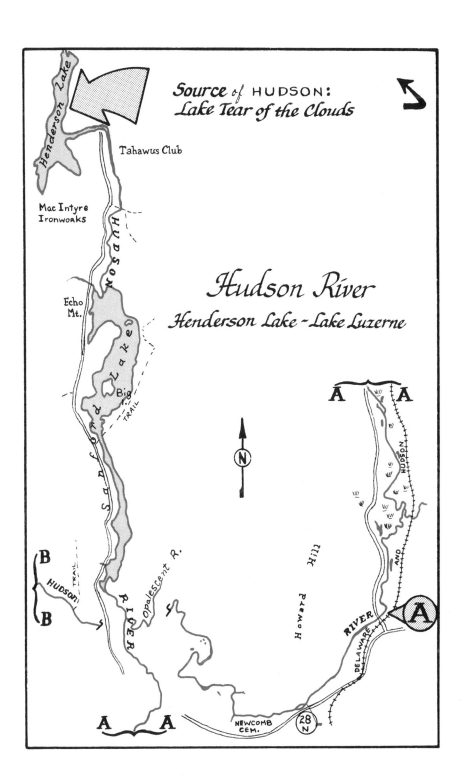

Source *of* HUDSON:
Lake Tear of the Clouds

Henderson Lake

Tahawus Club

Mac Intyre
Ironworks

Hudson

Hudson River
Henderson Lake – Lake Luzerne

Echo Mt.

Sanford Lake

Big
TRAIL

N

B

HUDSON
TRAIL

B

RIVER

Opalescent R.

Howard Hill

A   A

HUDSON   AND

A

RIVER

DELAWARE

A   A

NEWCOMB
CEM.

28
N

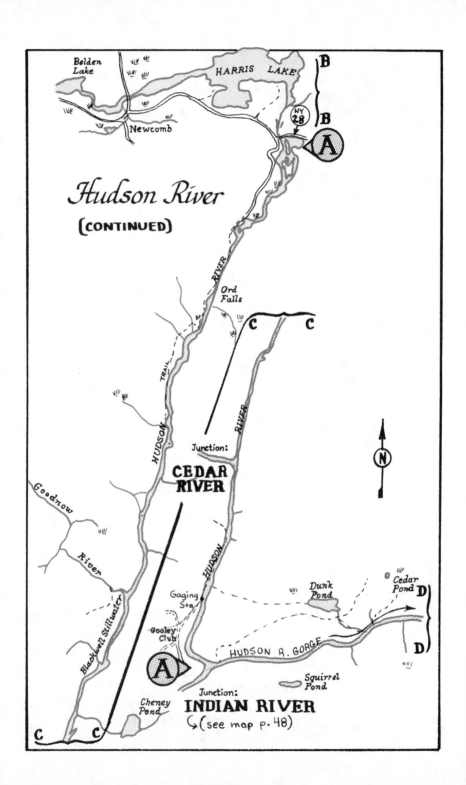

B

Belden Lake

HARRIS LAKE

NY 28

B

A

Newcomb

Hudson River

(CONTINUED)

RIVER

Ord Falls

C   **C**

TRAIL

RIVER

HUDSON

Junction:

CEDAR RIVER

Goodnow

River

HUDSON

Dunk Pond

Cedar Pond **D**

Gaging Sta.

Gooley Club

A

Blackwell Stillwater

HUDSON R. GORGE

D

Squirrel Pond

Cheney Pond

Junction:

INDIAN RIVER

↳ (see map p. 48)

C   **C**

N

After leaving Sanford Lake the narrow stream meanders, with only a slight drop, for a mile. Here the Opalescent River comes in on the left. From the junction of the Opalescent with the Hudson, the stream wanders for about five miles, dropping only sixteen feet to the bridge near the Tahawus Club and the road from Blue Ridge to Newcomb. It is seven miles from this bridge to the NY 28N bridge just east of Newcomb. The river drops 150 feet. One hundred feet of this drop is in the first mile and one-half. Consequently, you get Class III rapids, approaching Class IV, at six feet of water. The wise paddler will check ahead to see that the narrow channel is clear.

The stream joins the outlet of Harris Lake about three-tenths of a mile above the NY 28N bridge. Harris Lake Public Campsite is nearby.

NEWCOMB TO INDIAN RIVER JUNCTION

A good place to start a Hudson River trip is at the NY 28N bridge at Newcomb. The river is wide enough for easy passage and is also more accessible. After you leave Newcomb until you reach the Gooley Club, the roads and trails into the river are few and far between, and the lands are private and restricted. This section of the river involves a long shuttle. Leave a car at North River or the Gooley Club gate and go through Blue Mountain Lake and Long Lake villages to get to Newcomb.

There is an easy put-in and parking spot on the left bank down the river a few hundred feet from NY 28N. At first the river moves slowly, picks up speed going through a rocky chute called Long Falls, then after a couple of miles charges through Ord Falls, a Class III rapid. Ord Falls is not actually a falls but rather a steep chute where the 1520-foot contour crosses the river. You encounter some high waves when the water level on the North Creek gauge is 5.5 feet or higher, and if you have an open boat you may get swamped. However, if the bow paddler moves back of the front seat, or if both paddlers get in the middle, the boat has more rocker and will ride up over the high waves. Another helpful hint: If you back paddle like crazy, the bow will ride up and over the haystacks instead of charging through them.

After Ord Falls you drop slowly for three and one-half miles down to the Goodnow River, which comes in on the right. Below this the Blackwell Stillwater extends for a mile and a half. Here you may see some of the wildlife that lives in the area: deer, otter, beaver, mink and muskrats. Look back up the river to view the High Peaks of the

Adirondacks. To the right ahead you can see Cedar Mountain and Big Pisgah Mountain. There are some cottages on the left bank, accessible from a private road on the right bank which goes north to Newcomb. At the foot of the stillwater is the remains of an old splash dam used in logging drives to flush the logs down the river. Look this over. You may want to carry around it on the right bank. It can be rather tricky, depending on the water level.

For the next two miles the river drops more evenly. Then the Cedar River comes in on your right. Stop below the junction on the right bank and relax. The scenery is spectacular and the two rivers make an especially nice backdrop. Two and one-half miles down the lively river the Indian comes in on the right. Just before this you can see the buildings of the Gooley Club on the right bank among the trees. At the point between the two rivers you will find a path which leads up the hill to the road one-half mile away. From here it is about another one-half mile to the Gooley Club gate. Since this is a private club, you cannot drive beyond the gate without permission. Of course, if you are ready, willing and able you may want to proceed down through the Hudson River Gorge, one of the great river trips of the East. Just be sure you are able to handle Class V water.

HUDSON RIVER GORGE AND INDIAN RIVER

The Indian River from below Lake Abanakee and the Hudson River Gorge to North River is one of the most red-blooded trips in the State of New York. It is tops in white water, with everything from Class I rifts through to Class V rapids when the water is high. The gorge section should be attempted only by knowledgeable boaters.

Normally the best times for canoeing are from April to the middle of May and in September and October if the river level is right. The best level in this area for open canoes is when the reading on the gauge at North Creek is four to six feet. To get a river gauge reading you may call Pat Cunningham's Hudson River Rafting Company at 518-251-3215.

When the river is running at eight feet, the flow is 10,200 cubic feet per second (CFS). That is a powerful volume of water. A boater has no conception of this power until he has been caught, held under, and then spit out of a raging rapid. Pat likes to have his rafting guides go through exactly this experience in order to get a proper respect for the river.

In April and early May the water temperature of the Hudson River is about 40 degrees F. A wet suit is a must. A few years ago two young neophyte paddlers in T-shirts and shorts, and totally unprepared, attempted to raft the gorge. Due to the low temperatures of the air and water they developed hypothermia. When they reached North River, one was dead; the other spent weeks in the hospital recovering. Since 1980, the town fathers of Indian Lake have been releasing water from Indian Lake during May and June from 9:30 a.m. until 11:00 a.m. each day. In 1983 Fridays, Saturdays and Sundays from September 17th until October 15th were added to give the ten or so commercial rafters time to get up to eighty paying customers apiece afloat and carried down the river on the surge of water from the lake.

The gates on Lake Abanakee are opened to let the water through, resulting in an increase of about three feet in height on the Indian River. The surge spreads out more on the wider Hudson and increases its depth about six inches. The season is thus lengthened for the kayaker and canoer.

It is best to skip the Otter Slide, which starts at the foot of the Lake Abanakee Dam. In high water this is a Class V rapid, and it requires a rocky descent to reach. Two inexperienced kayakers once totalled both of their new kayaks within five minutes of each other here.

To reach the river, follow the Chain of Lakes Road north from NY 28 one mile east of Indian Lake Village. Drive .5 miles below the Lake Abanakee Dam, where you will find a natural draw on the right running down to the river. Be sure to park your vehicle so as not to block traffic on the road. You will, of course, already have placed a shuttle car at the Warren County Access area at North River, if this is your destination. This is about 15 miles and will take you about 4-5 hours actual travel time.

Put in at Rafter's Bay (Hudson Bay) at the foot of the draw where there is a pool for easy loading. You hardly get settled into the canoe when you hit Indian Head Rapids, a mile or so of Class III water when the full release is made. This is a great introduction to this wild river. The high water covers most of the rocks but makes for some high standing waves. A short raft will practically stand on end in them. The rapids are in such close proximity you barely recover from one of them before you are in the next.

After the Prying Islands comes the Gooley Steps, a series of staircases that continue for about three-quarters of a mile. Then the Indian flattens out as it joins the Hudson, and you have a quiet pool on which to rest. If you should have to leave the river, there is a trail at the point between the rivers which, after one-half mile, comes out on the Chain of Lakes Road. Follow this road southwest, or up the Indian River, to get back to NY 28 and Indian Lake. *See Map, p. 48.*

From the north edge of the river the boater can look up the Hudson and catch a glimpse of the Gooley Club, a private hunting and fishing club that leases 13,000 acres from the Finch Pruyn Paper Company. Below the junction of the Indian and the Hudson, the Hudson takes on an ominous character. It is fairly wide at this point, with rocky ledges on each side. The northern white cedar (arborvitae) growing on the ledges has a precise level line on the lower branches. It is as if a mighty landscaper had taken his hedge shears and trimmed the bottom of the limbs in a horizontal plane. My guess as to what caused this is that the deer stand on the ice on their hind legs and chew the lower branches as high as they can reach.

After passing Cedar Ledges, you drop into the dark and deep Black Hole. Three-quarters of a mile down the river, Elephant Rock shows up clearly on the left bank. After a left bend, you come to Duck Pond Flats, marked by the outlet from Duck Pond on the left bank. A mile farther on the left bank is Mink Falls. This beautiful 12-foot straight fall certainly deserves to have its picture taken. (Naturally, you will have your camera in a watertight case and have it fastened securely in the boat. You should never have anything loose in the boat.)

From Mink Falls it is three-tenths of a mile to Virgin Falls, the Huntley Pond Outlet, again on the left. You make a big half-mile sweep to the right, then turn left and start dropping fast. You are now in Blue Ledge Rapids, which end in a long pool beside the beautiful Blue Ledges. Be sure to stop on the left bank so you can properly admire the scenery.

The Ledges are a series of steps with more arborvitae growing on them. A DEC trail to the north leads out to Huntley Pond on the North Woods Club Road. Since you are out of your boat, you may want to hike down the river about 500 feet and look over the start of the Blue Ledge Narrows. The river is funnelled into a narrow passageway and becomes very turbulent. In high water this is a Class IV rapid.

After three-quarters of a mile of the Narrows you may feel ready for a rest. But hang on and go through the Class III Osprey Nest Rapid to Carter's Landing on the right opposite Split Rock. This is a good stopping point where there is room to stretch and rest. So far, the place has not been littered, even with the large numbers of people coming through on rafts. The rafting guides have done a fantastic job of keeping the area clean, even to the extent of picking up cigarette butts. Individual travelers would do well to follow their example.

After you leave the landing, you go about a mile and come to OK Slip Brook on the right. OK Slip Falls, a 100-plus drop, is worth the half-mile trip up the trail from the river. About two-tenths of a mile below the brook you arrive at Big Nasty, the Class IV Kettle Mountain Rapids that will test your skill. Terrific turbulence and waves buffet you from all directions. A quarter of a mile farther on you make a 90 degree turn to the left. If you now turn around and look to the west you will see a notch in the mountains that looks like a gun sight. This is called "gun sight in." In about one-fourth mile just before a right-hand turn you notice another notch on the eastern skyline. This is called "gun sight out."

After you make a 90 degree sweep to the right, you travel one-half mile and come to the worst rapids on the river—Harris Rift. It is best to scout the run. Land on the right bank. There is a huge rock in the river just left of center; if the water is going over the rock it is very dangerous because there is a really bad souse hole below the rock. Be sure to keep away from it and out of the hole.

Fortunately, at the foot of this rapid there is a large pool, so you can at least retrieve whatever floats down from the rapid and make whatever repairs are necessary with duct tape. A whitewater trip on a river such as this also necessitates wearing an approved helmet. Those rocks are there to stay!

After a respite in the pool below Harris Rift, the rest of the trip past Little Split Rock, the Bobcat's Den and the Fox Den is comparatively easy. When the Boreas Trestle (the Delaware & Hudson branch from the mines at Tahawus that follows alongside the Boreas River and crosses the Hudson a quarter of a mile above the junction of the two rivers) comes into view you quickly leave the gorge behind.

At the Boreas junction the river turns south again and you drift through Boreas Flats. Just when you think you are home free at about a mile and a quarter below Boreas Junction and just above Griffin Brook, a ledge crosses the river, making a two to three foot vertical drop with a resulting keeper hydraulic at the base. This is Bus Stop, and you certainly do stop at the foot of the drop. The trick is to keep going and get out of the keeper. Since early logging days this rapid had been known locally as the North River Black Hole.

Another mile below Griffin Brook Raquette Brook comes in on the right. The large Barton Mines processing plant also appears on the right. This plant processes into industrial abrasives the garnet which comes from nearby Gore Mountain.

The distance from this plant to Thirteenth Brook take-out is one and four-tenths miles. NY 28 comes down the hill from Indian Lake and parallels the river. Paddling beside the State highway, you come to the well-marked Warren County access area on the right bank at North River. You begin to unwind and realize the tension you were under coming through the fantastic Hudson River gorge. At North River you are finally and totally released from the gorge section of the Hudson.

NORTH RIVER TO HADLEY LUZERNE

From North River to Hadley Luzerne a canoer experiences the gamut of river difficulties, from Class I water in the section from Warrensburg to just above Hadley Luzerne to an impassable falls at Hadley Luzerne.

There are Class II rapids starting below the Perry Eller rapids at North River, the end of this run being at the D & H parking lot on the right at North Creek, and Class III from North Creek down to The Glen. When the water gauge at North Creek reads five to six feet, this is a great run.

At North River between NY 28 and the river are two Warren County Access Areas. From North River you can observe the Mouse's Tail across the river. Here, according to old timers, logs were released when the river level got up to the mouse's tail, a streak of black rock in the gray rock. Some say there is a speck of garnet at the end of the tail. Today, this tells the river runner that the level is good for running.

On the first weekend in May of each year the North Creek area is a very busy place. It is the location of the Hudson River White Water Derby with 500 or so contestants and an estimated 15,000 spectators. 1984 was the 27th annual running of the Derby. On Saturday there is a novice and a giant slalom open to all classes, open and closed boats, and to all ages. The novice race ends just above the Perry Eller rapids, and the giant slalom just below them. At high water the standing waves (haystacks) run about five to six feet high. With canoers crisscrossing back and forth, reversing and going upstream to get through the gates, this is a great spectacular.

From the rapids down to North Creek the river flows rather gently, giving you the opportunity to enjoy the Point of Rocks and the Whispering Pines. The hills rise higher and higher toward Gore Mountain to the west. About a mile before you reach North Creek a rivulet comes out of a keyhole in the rock above the left bank. At North Creek, after traveling five miles, you may pull in on the right bank at the parking lot just off the main street or continue down to Riparius.

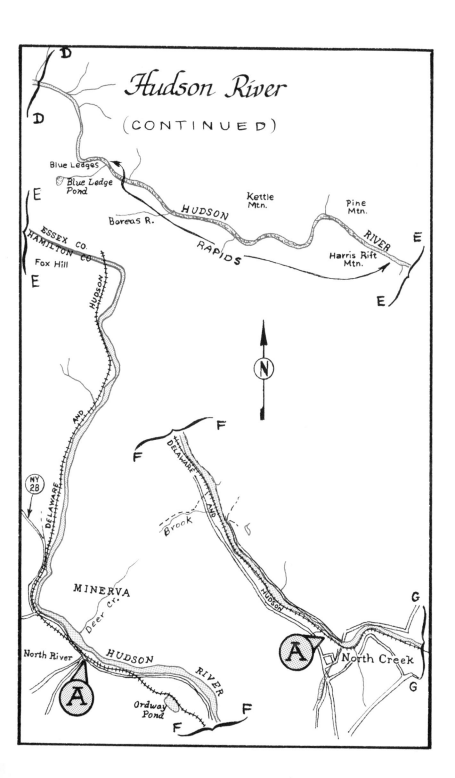

Hudson River

(CONTINUED)

Blue Ledges
Blue Ledge Pond
Kettle Mtn.
Pine Mtn.
HUDSON
Boreas R.
RIVER
RAPIDS
Harris Rift Mtn.
ESSEX CO.
HAMILTON CO.
Fox Hill
HUDSON
N
F
DELAWARE
AND
Brook
NY 28
DELAWARE
MINERVA
AND
Deer Cr.
HUDSON
G
North River
HUDSON
RIVER
A
North Creek
A
Ordway Pond
F
F
G

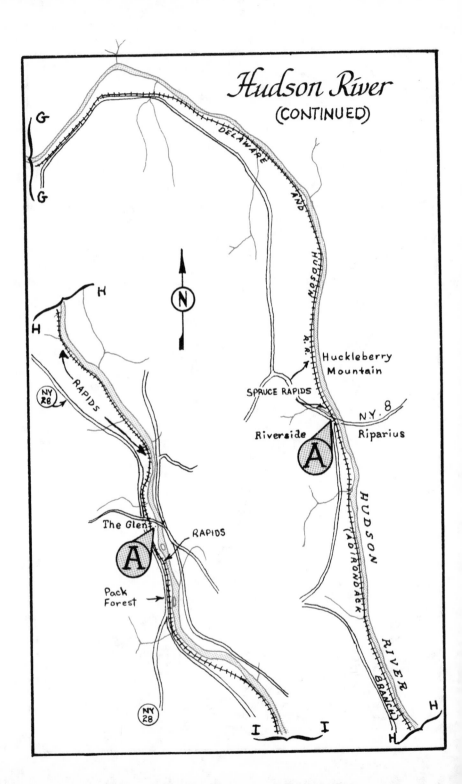

North Creek-Riparius is the course for the downriver race held on Sunday each year during the White Water Derby.

From the starting gate at North Creek you gain speed until you reach the NY 28N bridge where the USGS river gauge is located. Then you bend left and go down a little chute. From here the Delaware and Hudson Railroad, Adirondack Branch, is on the right bank all the way to Hadley, with the highway away from the river much of the way.

About three miles from the start there is a ledge across the river called Bird Pond Falls. From here on you find some lively water. Three miles below the ledge you come to the head of Spruce Rapids, the toughest rapids between North Creek and Riparius. It is a three-quarter mile section of Class III rapids when the river is running at five to six feet. I learned through experience that it is best to keep 30 to 50 feet off the left bank. Easy water at the foot of Spruce Rapids lets the adrenalin slow down before egressing at the Warren County Access Area on the right bank just below the NY 28 bridge.

The next section (Riparius to The Glen) has some fine white water. Two miles below the NY 8 bridge Mill Creek comes in on the right, adding to the volume of the water. The wilderness is delightful; you see no one except boaters.

About four-tenths of a mile below the creek there is a ledge across the river with about a three-foot drop. I once watched two of my friends in an open canoe come within 60 feet of this ledge when the water level was four and eight-tenths feet. To my amazement, they back-paddled and ferried acros the ledge until they picked the best spot to go through, which was left of center, then went over the ledge without difficulty. Before attempting to go through, stop and pick your route or carry around the ledge. At high water the hydraulic is powerful.

A half-mile below the ledge is Race Horse Rapids, a real Class III thriller. There is a good spot on the rocks on the left bank at the foot of these rapids to rest or picnic. Once, when exploring the banks above, I found two three-inch cables anchored in the rocks. Apparently a suspension bridge of some sort crossed the river at this point year ago.

A couple of miles below, the road comes close to the river and cars begin to show up on the left bank. As you approach The Glen NY 28 bridge an interesting chute is created when the river turns to the left, then curves back to the right. Except for one large rapid and several lesser ones in the next two miles downstream, this is the end of the white water section of the Hudson. A Warren County Access Area with parking facilities is on the right bank below the bridge. There is an unofficial water level gauge painted on the bridge.

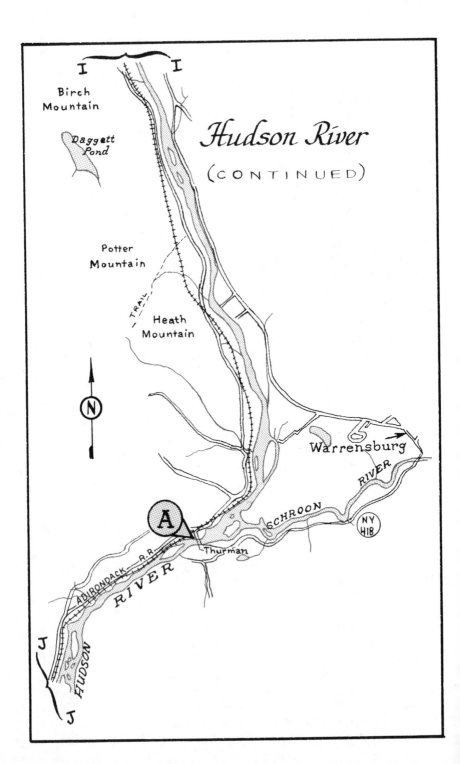

Birch
Mountain

Daggett
Pond

Hudson River

(CONTINUED)

Potter
Mountain

TRAIL

Heath
Mountain

N

Warrensburg

SCHROON   RIVER

NY
H18

A

ADIRONDACK   R.R.

Thurman

HUDSON   RIVER

J

J

I   I

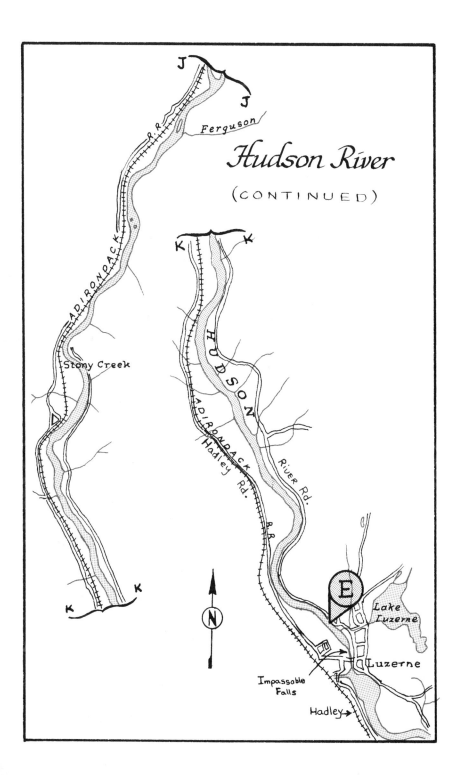

For an easier section of the river, you may proceed down the stream eight and five-tenths miles to the NY 418 bridge where the Schroon River joins the Hudson on the left. Warrensburg is three miles up the Schroon from this junction. Starting from the NY 28 bridge at The Glen, it is one-half mile to the last heavy water in this section, a ledge with a two and one-half foot drop on the right of center and considerable turbulence. Going through the center of the rapid I expected to be tossed about, but at the four and eight-tenths foot water level, in a closed boat, I had no problem. You can escape the rough water by keeping left or by lining the boat down the left side of the stream. From here on the river flattens and widens and you shouldn't have any difficulty. In fact, you may have trouble getting over the rifts and shoals if the water is low. This part of the stream is subject to ice jams, and you will find trees debarked by the ice at levels up to fifteen feet above the normal flow of the stream.

The Pack Forest, operated by the College of Forestry and Environmental Science at Syracuse University, bounds the river on the left bank for a quarter of a mile. A visit to the headquarters on US 9 and a walk through the large white pines provide a nice change of pace.

As you go on down the river there are some glacial moraines covered with white pines which make good places to pause for a picnic or a rest. NY 28 follows along the left bank for about five miles, and there is a gravel road close to the river on the right bank all the way to Thurman, a former hamlet, at the NY 418 bridge. There is a take-out on the right bank just below the bridge. Below Thurman you find more flat water and several large islands in the river where you might like to camp.

Six miles below Thurman, Stony Creek comes in on the right. Seven and one-half miles below Stony Creek, start looking for the access site on the left bank. This is the end of your trip, since the Hadley Luzerne Falls are about three-quarters of a mile below. These falls are *very* dangerous and should not be approached. When you park your shuttle car at the aforementioned access site at the beginning of your trip, you should pick out the landmarks so you can identify the spot easily from the river. In 1983 one good landmark was a three-foot diameter northern white cedar (arborvitae) on the bank of the access site. It is the largest tree of that species I have ever seen.

Though you don't approach the falls by canoe, you will want to see them from the bridge between Luzerne and Hadley. There is a park that extends up along the falls on the left bank. From the bridge and looking downstream you can see the Sacandaga River coming in on the right.

INDIAN RIVER

Indian River

Tributary: Hudson River

County: Hamilton

U.S.G.S. Maps: 15-minute 1/62500
Indian Lake, Blue Mountain, Newcomb

Total Length: 17.5 mi.

Cruising Length: Indian River 3 mi.;
Indian Lake 12 mi.; Jessup River 1.5 mi.;
Miami River 1 mi.

Season Recommended: River—April-May;
Lakes—All seasons

Campsites: Lewey Lake Public Campsite

Access	Location	Elev. Feet	Distance Miles	Inter. Dist.	Drop Feet	Gradient Ft./Mile	Rating Class
	Indian Lake — Jessup River						
	Source: Jessup River SW of Perkins Clearing	2,190	34.4				
				13.7	528	40	
	NY 10 Bridge	1,662	21.7				
				1.5	12	8	I
	Inlet Indian lake	1,650	20.2				
				12			I
A	Outlet Indian Lake	1,650	8.2				
				4.9			III-IV
A	Outlet Lake Abanakee	1,598	3.3				
				3.3			III-IV
E	Jct. Hudson River		0				
	Lewey Lake — Miami River						
	Source: Miami River S of Pillsbury Mt.	2,700	11	9.3	1,050	100	
	Inlet Lewey Lake	1,650	1.7				
				1.7			I
A	Outlet Lewey Lake	1,650	0				

Indian Lake

Boisterous Indian River flows out of Indian Lake, located in the east-central section of Hamilton County, NY. Almost fourteen miles long and nearly a mile wide, the lake extends from two miles south of the village of Indian Lake, with NY 30 along the western edge, to a point about seven miles north of Speculator. Its maximum depth is eighty feet. Lake trout, small-mouth bass, whitefish, northern pike, and a few brown trout and landlocked salmon live in its waters.

Lewey Lake Campsite, with 215 sites, is on the southwest arm of the lake. There is a public launching ramp on Indian Lake within the campsite where you can apply for campsite permits on the islands in Indian Lake. Each campsite has a fireplace, a table and a pit toilet.

There are many islands and bays to explore on the lake. The inlet arm of the lake below the Jessup River is about six miles long. We once were entertained for about ten minutes on this arm by an otter, a real clown, who would dive, catch a fish, bring it up and show it to us, repeating the performance three times. We had a ball watching him.

The Jessup River, which starts west of NY 30 above Perkins Clearing, flows into this arm of the lake. You can go down the Jessup if the water is high. Turn off NY 30 just north of Mason Lake and go into Perkins Clearing. There is a nice campsite by the old bridge. There may be log jams and debris to clear in order to get down the stream. The river flows east and north under NY 30, and about one-half mile beyond flows into the lake. Because the lake is so long, the wind can kick up some high waves. Beware of this.

A high dam at the lower end of the lake raises the water about thirty-three feet above the former lake level. During the spring of 1983, releases from the dam were made from 9:30 a.m. to 11 a.m. daily. In the fall they were made only on weekends. These releases are made to provide good levels of water for canoeing and rafting on the Indian and Hudson rivers.

Indian River below Lake Abanakee is described in the Hudson River section. See *Hudson River Gorge and Indian River, p. 32 ff.*

Lewey Lake

One and a half-mile-long Lewey Lake is across the highway (NY 30) from Indian Lake and flows directly into it. When Indian Lake is full the two lakes are the same level, but late in the summer there may be a foot or two difference. When this happens you line your canoe from one lake to the other, or you portage over the highway. Lewey Lake

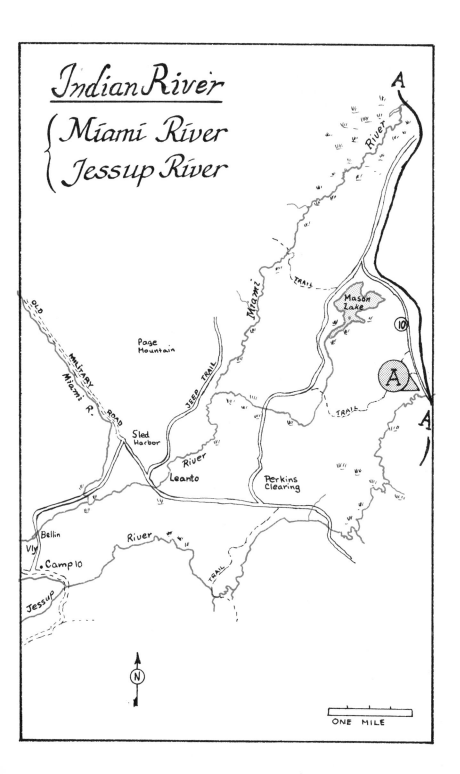

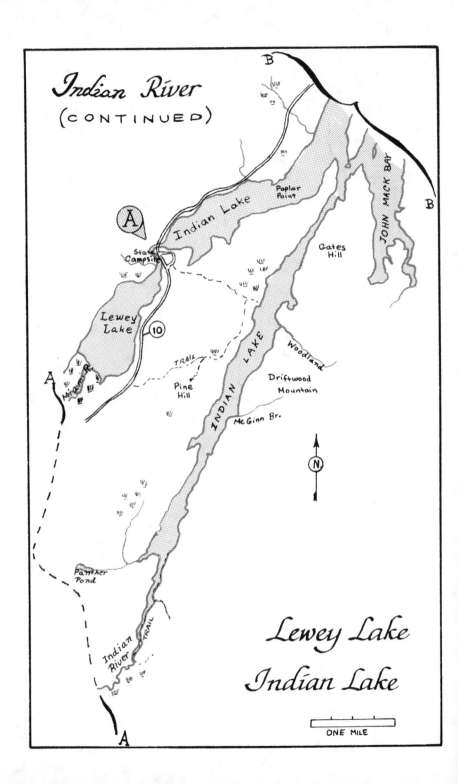

Indian River
(CONTINUED)

B

Indian Lake

Poplar Point

JOHN MACK BAY

Gates Hill

A

State Campsite

Lewey Lake

10

Woodland

INDIAN LAKE

Driftwood Mountain

A'

Miami R.

TRAIL

Pine Hill

McGinn Br.

N

B

Panther Pond

Indian River

TRAIL

A

Lewey Lake

Indian Lake

ONE MILE

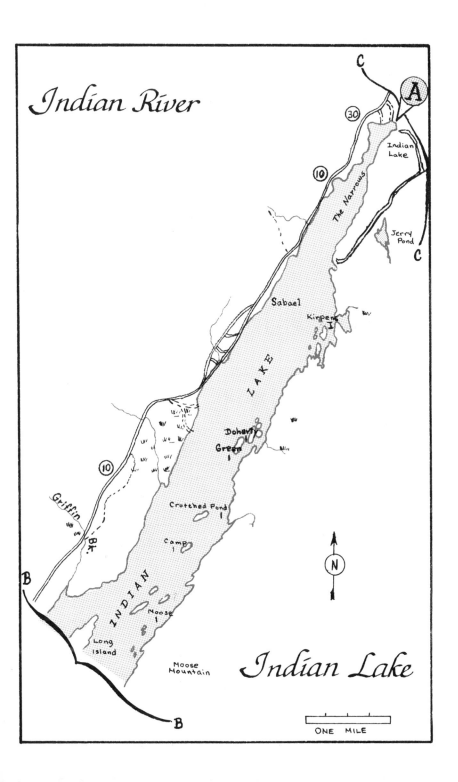

Indian River

Indian Lake

Jerry Pond

The Narrows

Sabael

Kirpens I

Doherty Green

Crotched Pond

Camp

Moose I

Long Island

INDIAN LAKE

Moose Mountain

Griffin Bk.

Indian Lake

N

ONE MILE

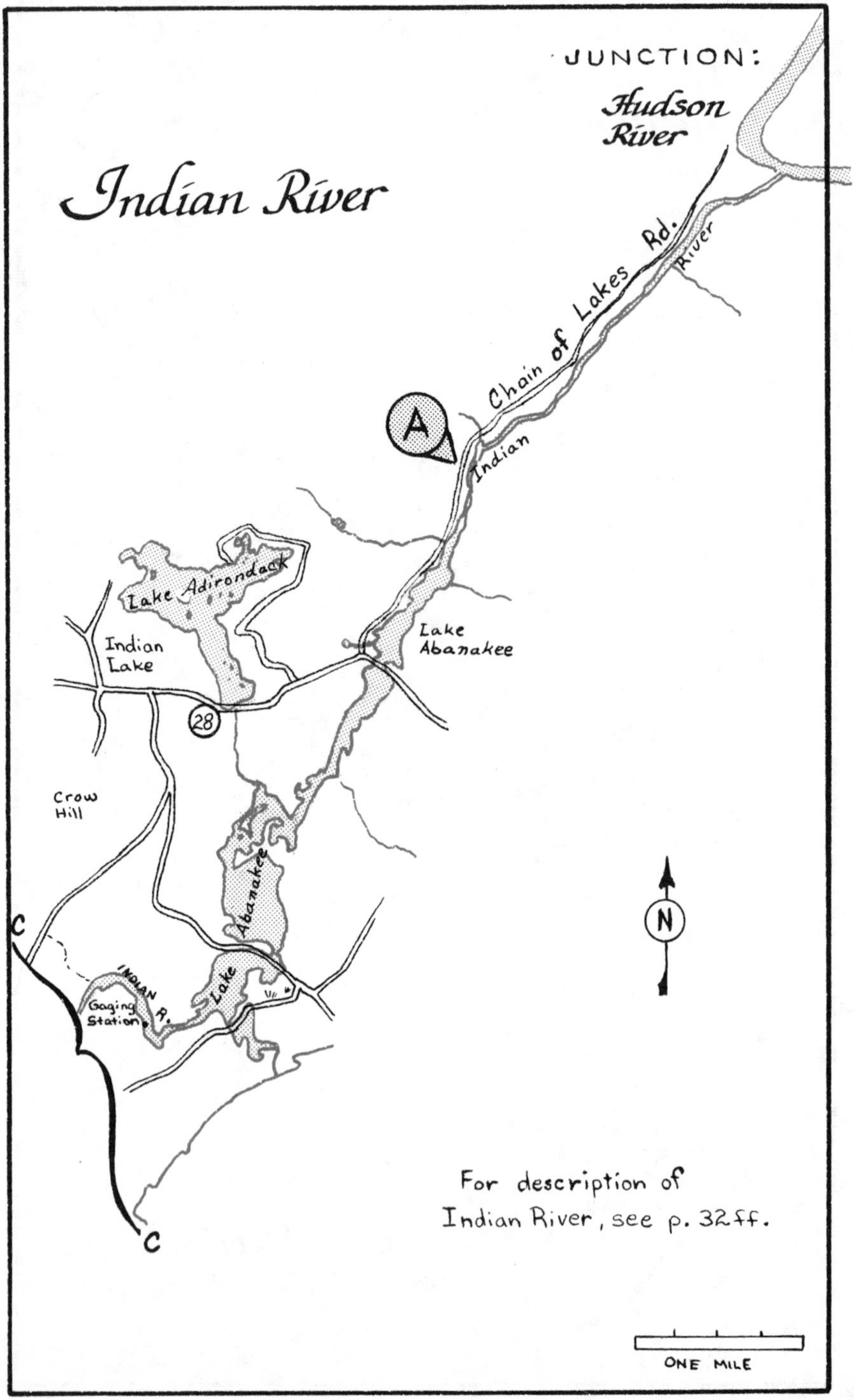

JUNCTION:
Hudson River

Indian River

Chain of Lakes Rd.

Indian River

(A)

Indian

Lake Adirondack

Indian Lake

Lake Abanakee

(28)

Crow Hill

Lake Abanakee

C

INDIAN R.

Gaging Station

Lake Abanakee

Up

N

C

For description of
Indian River, see p. 32ff.

ONE MILE

Public Campsite, which is on both sides of the lake, has both a launching site and a bathing beach. From Snowy Mountain, elevation 3903 feet, you can get a fantastic view of the lakes and the high mountains to the north. The Snowy Mountain Trail is marked from NY 30 south of Sabael.

The Miami River, which parallels NY 10 and the Jessup River Road, flows into Lewey Lake. The inlet is found about in the middle of the south end of the lake and has canoeable water for over a mile. The beavers here are very active, and it will be necessary to pull your canoe over their dams in order to go up the river. The pine and balsam knolls along the way make excellent picnic sites. They are covered with bracken, evergreen wood ferns, bunchberry and gold thread. Beautiful royal ferns grow along the banks.

KUNJAMUK RIVER

Kunjamuk River

Tributary: Sacandaga River	**Total Length:** 17.5 mi.
County: Hamilton	**Cruising Length:** 5.5 mi.
U.S.G.S. Maps: 15-minute 1/62500 Indian Lake	**Season Recommended:** All of canoeing season
	Campsites: Sacandaga Public Campsite, Moffitt Beach Public Campsite

Access	Location	Elev. Feet	Distance Miles	Inter. Dist.	Drop Feet	Gradient Ft./Mile	Rating Class
	South Pond	2,310	17.5	17.5	586	33	
	Old Barrier Dam	1,750	9.5				
				6	22	4	I
	Elm Lake	1,728	3.5				
				3.5	4	1	I
A	Jct. Sacandaga - Kunjamuk Bay NY 8 east of Speculator at State Marker 1296	1,724	0				

The tranquil Kunjamuk River is one of the more delightful little waterways of the Adirondacks. Every Adirondack canoe explorer should paddle it at least once.

The best place to start a trip up the Kunjamuk is at the launching site on Kunjamuk Bay at NY 8 State marker 1296. This now has a "Canoe Access" sign. An alternate access is the outlet of Lake Pleasant by the NY 8 bridge in Speculator at the south end of the main street. It adds a 1.6 mile trip down the Sacandaga to Kunjamuk Bay. Personally, I feel the time saved by putting into Kunjamuk Bay can be better spent exploring above Elm Lake along the river. Another alternative, which

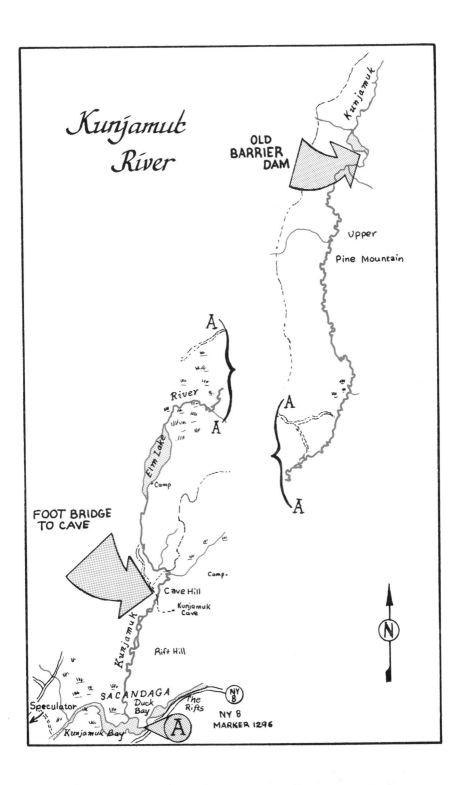

requires a shuttle or a hired vehicle, is to go north from the four corners in Speculator. One way is to take the first right turn beyond the paved road (in 1983) about one-quarter mile, then keep left at the next two intersections. This brings you to a large gravel bank and a ramp into the Elm Lake Outlet.

To canoe up the river start from Kunjamuk Bay and follow the winding river back and forth. Because the water is deep the paddling is easy. The beaver are alive and thriving on the Kunjamuk. The last time we were there, in early September 1983, we crossed seven beaver dams (four were active) and one log jam on the stream before reaching Elm Lake. The series of four dams raised the water level approximately five, eight, ten and fifteen inches respectively. The trip took one and one-half hours to go the three and one-half miles.

The stream banks were lined with the fruits of the season. The bright red of the American high bush cranberry was the most spectacular; the many-colored wild raisin was the thickest. The berries ranged from green to white to pink to red, and a few were turning the deep purple of complete ripeness. Also on the banks were red osier, elderberry and pannicled (grey) dogwood. The purple pickerel weed was in bloom in the bays, along with a few white pond lilies. The prettiest flower of all was the aquatic form of swamp smartweed. These delicate pink spikes of the buckwheat family with their floating leaves were close to the shores of Elm Lake.

Paddling up Elm Lake (length .8 mi.) we enjoyed the view of the misty mountains in the distance. The inlet was deep and meandering. As soon as we came to shallower water and the stream bed, the beaver were in evidence. We saw one go underwater. Apparently he didn't see us, for he started swimming downstream toward us. When he discovered us, looking like a leviathan coming upstream on a collision course with him, he up-ended and with a terrific splash of his tail took off for less crowded waters.

In the next mile we crossed twelve beaver dams and nine log jams. The alder was catching the upper ends of our paddles as the waterway closed in to about four feet in width. At this point we decided it was judicious to go back downriver to the Sacandaga. By actual count we crossed fifty-four obstructions in the river that day. Going to Elm Lake the dams were helpful; above Elm Lake the river is so full of snags, dams and drowned trees it is laborious at best.

On the way back we stopped at the foot bridge and followed the trail east to Kunjamuk Cave. A sign on old Route 8 tells of a prospector starting a mine shaft here and forming the cave. A skylight in the cave helps you see the interior, which goes back nearly twenty feet. On a previous trip we saw a black bear cross the river near the footbridge. This day, as we looked out over the marsh at the outlet of Elm Lake, a faint light from a wingbeat caught our eyes, then a darting spot of white appeared, then disappeared, then reappeared. We got to where we could see it clearly, see its fantastic gyrations in the air—hovering then diving for prey—and we knew it could be only one thing: the marsh hawk, one of nature's great stunt flyers.

From one of the natives we learned about the early log drives on the river. A barrier dam was constructed where the logs were collected, later to be flushed down the stream during the high water in the spring. The dam was located near the edge of State land and close to the outlet (Cisco Brook) of Owl Lake. The log drives ended about 1920, and for some time after that the river was open. Gradually the alders closed in, the beaver dams were built, and log jams developed, so that today the upper stream is a real obstacle course.

But the lower section remains a treat. Go, see, and enjoy.

MOOSE RIVER

FULTON CHAIN OF LAKES

The Fulton Chain of Lakes was named after Robert Fulton, who was commissioned in the early 1800s by the State of New York to see if a water route could be built from the Erie Canal to the St. Lawrence River. Apparently he did not deem the route feasible, for he never filed a report.

The Middle Branch of the Moose River starts at the outlet of the Fulton Chain of Lakes. Because most canoers proceed up the chain from First Lake at Old Forge, a popular resort village, to Eighth Lake, I will describe them in that order, though the flow is in the opposite direction.

Originally, there were eight separate lakes in the Fulton Chair. After John Brown (not the abolitionist) built the first dam at Old Forge, the waterway became continuous from First Lake through Fifth Lake. The launching site in Old Forge is between the dam and the village information building. From the launch site, you paddle northeastward along the channel approximately one and one-half miles to where First Lake widens to about a mile. There are many cottages on the north shore, but few on the south.

After going one mile you pass De Camp Island on the right, after which you will be in Second Lake. Bearing toward the north for one mile, you will discover the opening to Third Lake. After another mile in a northerly direction, you will find a passageway through into Fourth Lake.

You have now traveled four and one-half miles and entered the largest lake in the chain, which is five and one-half miles long. Because of this lake's exposed location, you should be careful not to get caught in high winds when canoeing on it.

Moose River
including Middle Branch and Fulton Chain of Lakes

Tributary: Black River

Counties: Hamilton, Herkimer, Lewis, Oneida

U.S.G.S. Maps: 15-minute 1/62500
Raquette Lake, Big Moose, West Canada Lakes; Old Forge, McKeever
7.5-minute 1/24000
Port Leyden

Total Length: 45.5 mi.

Cruising Length: 43 mi.

Season Recommended: April-Mid-May, Summer releases

Campsites: Nicks Lake Public Campsite, Limekiln Public Campsite, Eighth Lake Public Campsite

Access	Location	Elev. Feet	Distance Miles	Inter. Dist.	Drop Feet	Gradient Ft./Mile	Rating Class
	East end Eighth Lake and portage to Brown Tract Pond outlet	1,791	45.5				
				1.5			I
A	Eighth Lake	1,791	44				
				2	5	2	
A	Seventh Lake	1,786	43				I
				3	1		
A	Sixth Lake	1,785	40				
				.5			
	Portage N end of Fifth Lake	1,707	39.5				
A	Fourth Lake		33.5				
	Third Lake		32.5	10.5	0	0	I
	Second Lake		31.5				
	First Lake	1,707	30.5				
A	Above Dam at Old Forge	1,707	29				
				1	15	15	III
A	Jct. North and Middle Branches	1,692	28				
				9.5	184	19	III
	Jct. South and Middle Branches	1,508	18.5				
				1.5	16	10	III
A	McKeever Bridge NY 28	1,492	17				
				.5	3	6	II
A	Gauging Station	1,489	16.5				
				3.3	38	10	III
A	Moose River (Iron Bridge)	1,451	13.2				
				8.2	267	33	IV
A	Fowlersville	1,184	5				
				2	112	56	IV-V
A	Lyonsdale	1,072	3				
				1.3	132	100	IV-V
E	Power Line Rapids	940	1.7				
	Jct. Black River at Lyons Falls	800	0				

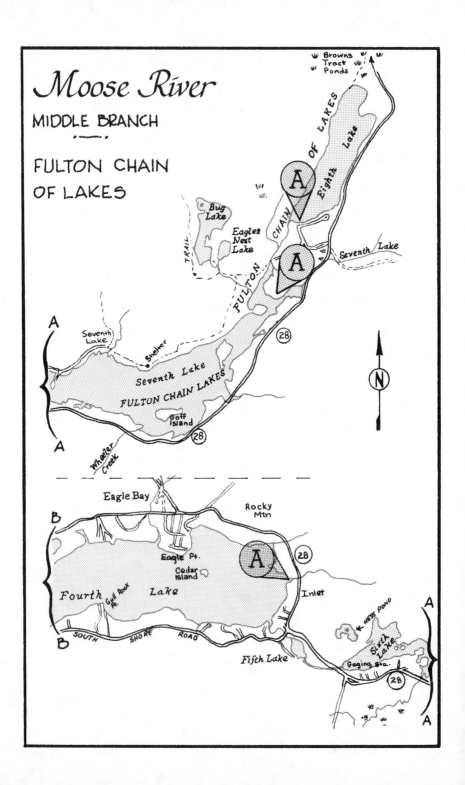

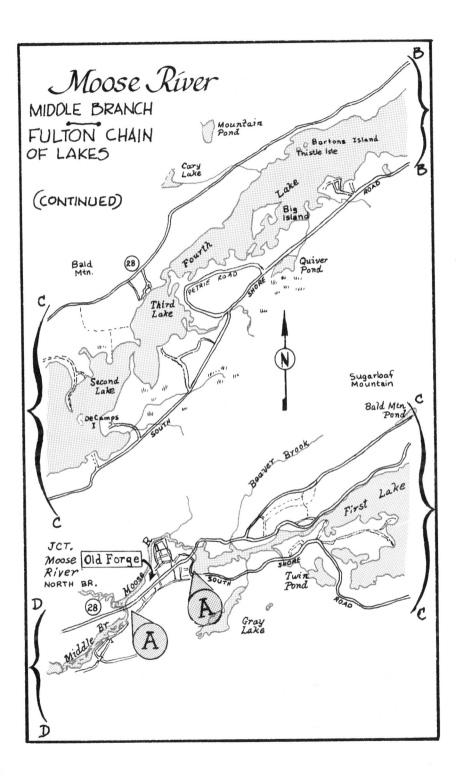

Moose River

MIDDLE BRANCH

FULTON CHAIN
OF LAKES

(CONTINUED)

Going north for one and one-half miles, you come to Big Island as shown on the USGS sheet, now called Alger Island. The Department of Environmental Conservation maintains a public campsite here with a caretaker in charge. There are fifteen lean-tos available for a fee ($5.50 for six people in 1983). The island is well-maintained with good fireplaces, pit toilets, and nice trails beneath giant white pines and mixed hardwoods.

South of the island on the mainland off the South Shore Road, which goes from Old Forge to Inlet, the DEC maintains a parking and picnic site and a launching area.

From Alger (Big) Island you go northeastward to Inlet, the village at the head of Fourth Lake. A New York State fishing access site is located here between the lake and NY 28. If you look closely, you will find the inlet just south of the access area (about 400 feet). On this half-mile channel there is a marina where you can stop to shop, or you might want to visit the village of Inlet.

The channel opens into Fifth Lake, which is only about one-fourth of a mile long and dotted with white pond lilies during the summer months. From here, you follow a winding stream speckled with both red and white elderberry bushes. Rather appropriately, I found a four-inch moosewood tree growing here, on the banks of the Moose, its showy green bark streaked with white.

Upon reaching an old iron bridge, you land on the right, or north, bank. There is a portage up the path 300 feet to NY 28. Here you turn right along the highway, then left along the blacktop road up to the dam on Sixth Lake. Highway signs mark the carry of seven-tenths of a mile. When you reach the highway, remember that with your head up in the canoe, you will not hear or see as well as you would otherwise. Use caution while walking.

Put in on the north shore opposite Bird's Flying Service and go east one mile to the steel bridge, where you pass into Seventh Lake. From here it is about two and one-half miles to the boat launching site at the head of Seventh Lake.

The eastern half of this lake is all on State land, with the line going mid-way through the largest island (Goff) in the lake. There are many camping sites on the north shore, including two lean-tos about mid-way up the lake. There is also one lean-to on the island.

Another possible access is the New York State launching site located on the south shore adjacent to NY 28.

Under proper water conditions, you can follow up the north channel at the end of the lake to Bug Lake Trail, thereby cutting your portage in half. Otherwise, take out on the ramp at Eighth Lake Campsite, which extends from Seventh Lake to Eighth Lake (there are 121 campsites available). The carry through the campsite is one mile long. Put into Eighth Lake at the launching site. The paddle is one and one-half miles to the upper end of Eighth Lake, which is surrounded by State land and is the only lake in the chain without private cottages. There are lean-tos on the lake, with one on the island mid-way up the lake. At the north end, you can carry out to NY 28 where the lake is plainly visible from the highway.

This is the end of the Fulton Chain of Lakes, but it is only a gateway to the extensive waterways to the north. If you take the marked carry from the end of Eighth Lake, after one and one-tenths miles you come out on the Brown Tract Ponds outlet (inlet on the USGS sheet). From here it is two and one-half miles to Raquette Lake, and from there you can go up the Marion River to Blue Mountain Lake by way of the Marion River Carry, Utowana Lake, and Eagle Lake. To go down the Raquette River, cross Raquette Lake to Forked Lake, down the Raquette River through Long Lake, then on down the Raquette River to Axton.

At Axton, you go right via Stony Creek Ponds and Indian Carry to Saranac Lakes. Otherwise, you can go down the Raquette River to Tupper Lake and from there on down the Raquette to the St. Lawrence.

For more information about these rivers, see Paul Jamieson's guide, *Adirondack Canoe Waters, North Flow*, published by the Adirondack Mountain Club.

MIDDLE BRANCH

The Middle Branch of the Moose starts at the outlet of the Fulton Chain of Lakes at the municipal beach and Chamber of Commerce Information Center in Old Forge. It courses along the north edge of the village of Old Forge and in the one-mile run to the junction of the North Branch of the Moose drops fifteen feet. There is access to the river on the right bank just below the NY 28 bridge between Old Forge and Thendara, but parking is lacking. A safer access is down the left bank about one-tenth mile below the bridge.

At the junction the river becomes placid as it winds its way under the NY 28 bridge and meanders for a couple of miles down to the "lock and dam," so called because it was just that in the early 1800s when the river was the first mode of travel. Boats, including the side-wheeler *Fawn* (see Lower Moose section), carried people and their goods from Onekio to Thendara, at that time called Fulton Chain.

This is a peaceful part of the river. We once startled a mother wood duck and her brood of five here. They skittered off in different directions, with the mother crying *weep...weep...weep*. Later, a pair of red-winged blackbirds protested loudly from a grassy island when we came too close to their nest. Then, just below, we came to a six-foot-high beaver house with a small wooden ladder running to the peak. Probably high water had lodged it there, but it looked as if the beaver might have been checking his roof. About here you can also see the old Utica-Malone Division of the New York Central Railroad, built by Col. William Webb in the 1800s. It not only provided public service but also gave him access to Lake Lila and his summer home.

The eight-foot dam has a lower spillway on the right hand end, so as the water drops the flow will be deeper over the right end than it would be if the spillway were on one level. When you get to the dam, carry around it on either end. There is a makeshift fireplace on the right bank and a road leading out to the highway.

Below the dam the river wanders from one side of the valley to the other. On this section we once saw a muskrat swimming across the stream and a bit further on, a common merganser with eight young. Nature was particulary good to us that June day. The spicy aroma of pink azalea (pinkster) came up the river and prepared us for the beautiful display of flowers around the bend. Highbush cranberry (one of the viburnums) with its two types of flowers was in full bloom along both sides of the river, and we were serenaded by yellow throated warblers and the "peabody, peabody, peabody" of white throated sparrows.

When you see the microwave tower on Flat Rock Mountain you come into the first rapids (Class II), and soon after you pass the little settlement of Minnehaha on the right bank. One-tenth of a mile below Minnehaha you come to Singing Waters Campground, where there is good access on the right bank. This is the site of the White Water Race held each October. The Slalom race is held on Saturday, the downriver race on Sunday. The downriver race course is from the campground down to the McKeever bridge. A good spot for viewing the downriver race is just below the gauging station on the right bank of the Moose. Park by the gravel pit about two miles above McKeever and two miles below Singing Waters, walk down to the railroad tracks, then go downstream along the tracks until you come to the roughest part of the river.

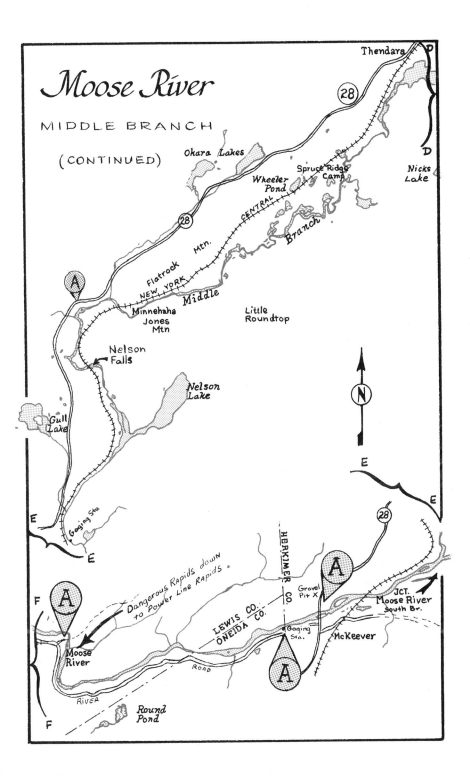

Moose River
MIDDLE BRANCH
(CONTINUED)

Thendara

28

Okara Lakes

Spruce Ridge Camp

D

D

Nicks Lake

Wheeler Pond

28

CENTRAL

Branch

A

Flatrock Mtn.

NEW YORK

Middle

Minnehaha
Jones Mtn

Little Roundtop

Nelson Falls

Nelson Lake

N

Gull Lake

Gaging Sta.

E

E

E

E

28

E

E

Dangerous Rapids down to Power Line Rapids

HERKIMER CO.

Gravel Pit X

A

JCT.
Moose River
South Br.

F

A

LEWIS CO.
ONEIDA CO.

Gaging Sta.

A

McKeever

Moose River

ROAD

A

RIVER

Round Pond

F

Below Singing Waters Campground the water starts dropping fast through a boulder-strewn streambed. An upset is likely if you misjudge the best route. About a mile below Singing Waters is a 500-foot portage starting just above the railroad trestle. Take out on the right bank, follow the railroad, then take a path on the left back to the river. This portage is around Nelson Falls, a Class IV rapid. It has been run by advanced paddlers when the water conditions were ideal.

In April and the first part of May, depending on the run-off, and in October when there is a release from the Fulton Chain of Lakes, the medium high water makes this section a very exciting Class II and Class III run, with the exception of Nelson Falls. The water is fast, and the run is especially exciting for an open canoe.

About one-half mile below the gauging station the South Branch of the Moose joins on the left and forms the Moose River. It is two miles from here to the McKeever bridge, where there is an access on the right bank just above the bridge. An easier egress, though, is one-half mile downstream on the left bank at another gauging station.

LOWER MOOSE

The section of the Moose River from McKeever down to Fowlersville is known as the Lower Moose. This third progression of the river is twelve miles long. It has Class IV water with several difficult runs to be undertaken only by advanced paddlers.

The best access to the Lower Moose is by the gauging station located one-half mile down the Moose River Road from the McKeever bridge. You may call 518-465-3491 to get the reading on this gauge. The first set of dings you hear is for feet, the second for tenths of a foot, and the third for hundredths of a foot. As you put into the water, you can read the gauge yourself. The river is runnable when the gauge reads between two and four feet.

From the gauging station you travel about one-half mile over placid water, then come to a rift full of boulders. A little farther, steep rock faces show up on the right. Here you plunge into a Class III rapid. You see a huge rock on your left, so big, in fact, that the 200-yard run is named for it: Big House Rock Rapids. Next, the river splits around an island where you go right to catch a two-and-a-half ft. vertical drop.

Moose River, a former hamlet that is now only a wide place in the road suitable for camping, shows up next. Just below is an old iron bridge which used to be the Moose River crossing for people from

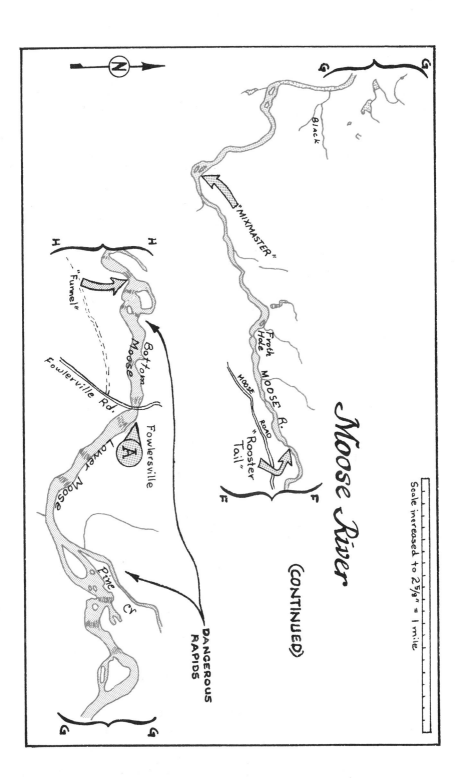

Moose River
(CONTINUED)

N

Scale increased to 2⅝" = 1 mile

Black

"MIXMASTER"

Froth Hole

MOOSE R.

MOOSE ROAD

"Rooster Tail"

"Funnel"

Bottom Moose

Fowlerville Rd.

Fowlersville

A

Lower Moose

Pine Cr.

DANGEROUS RAPIDS

G G
H H
F F
G G

Utica and the south who were headed toward Old Forge. This was a many-faceted trip. Travelers first were pulled by horses up the Remsen Road through Boonville to Moose River, then across the old iron bridge to board the Peg Leg Railroad, a three-foot-wide gauge railroad with wooden rails fastened to a corduroy road. The passenger car was an open-air affair with wooden benches. It ran in the summer only, and if the track was wet the passengers had to get off and push the train up the grades. The Peg Leg traveled to Onekio on the Moose River near present day Minnehaha. There, the traveler again changed his mode of travel and boarded the *Fawn*, a side-wheeler, shallow draught boat which carried him up the river through lock and dam to Fulton Chain, now called Thendara.

The Lower Moose starts dropping fast after you pass under the iron bridge, and the first rock band going all the way across the river shows up. The ledge pattern prevails on the remainder of the river. The Iron Bridge Rapids has Class III water and two vertical drops. Next, you reach Tannery Rapids, named after an old tannery, the foundation of which can still be seen on the left bank. There are two ledges in Tannery, one with about a four-foot drop, the other about six feet. Here the river drops forty feet in less than a half mile. At this point the road leaves the river for eight miles, till the Fowlersville road crosses the river at Fowlersville.

Following Tannery Rapids is Rooster Tail, perhaps the most exciting rapid on the river. First you think you have come through a Class IV rapid, but then the waves start buffeting you from all directions and you realize you are in the middle of a rooster tail for sure.

Two miles below Iron Bridge comes Froth Hole. Hit it dead center unless there is high water. When the water is high, go to the left. There is an excellent "lunch rock" here (L) sloping to the water. It is important to avoid the right as there is a vertical drop right onto a rock. More than one boat has been split in half here. An article in *Canoe Magazine* (July-August 1975) called this an "impassable" rapid.

About a mile down the river comes Mixmaster, a Class V rapid successfully run only by very experienced paddlers. The first hole stops you; the second can tear you up. One fellow literally had his clothes torn off his body in this maelstrom. To avoid it take out on the right bank.

After passing a large island on the left, you come to Elevator Shaft. There is a possible pin situation here if there is low volume. The greatest volume of water goes down a chute near the right bank. When the water is high, you go down the chute, do a backender, and, under the right conditions, are propelled out of the water — a boat airborne. The few more chutes before you come to the Fowlersville bridge are anti-climactic. As you take out on the right bank, you say to yourself, "Ah! I've conquered the Lower Moose."

BOTTOM MOOSE

The Bottom Moose has always been considered separate from the Lower Moose because it has not been canoed until recently. With the improvements in the state of the art, and canoers today being more adept and more daring than in the past, it is no longer considered unrunnable. It is definitely not for everyone, however. Look it over carefully before tackling it and make sure you can handle it.

The 3.3-mile stretch of the Bottom Moose goes from Fowlersville Bridge down to Power Line Rapids just above Crystal Falls. Power Line Rapids shows on the Port Leyden Quadrangle USGS map as a white slash with two broken lines running through, just upriver from Kosterville.

Starting on the lower side of the Fowlersville bridge is a 48-foot slide into shallow water. It is an elbow breaker, and a good place to avoid.

About a half mile below the bridge, the river narrows and goes through a chute called the Funnel. At the bottom of the Funnel is a diamond-splitting rock. You must go to the right of this rock. At the top of the funnel is a souse hole. If you fail to punch through it you will be in trouble.

After the Funnel comes Knife Edge. You should not try to run this because there is a tree across the stream. Portage around it.

Another mile below this you come to Upper Lyondale. You can see the Lyondale bridge from this spot. There are two drops here totaling about twelve feet. Run to the left of center on the tongue and into a big hole at the bottom. Once you reach bottom the river spits you out like a recalcitrant child spitting out spinach. I saw one canoer dumped and held in the hole for several seconds before he was able to overcome the pull of the hydraulic. When he finally caught up with his covered canoe, he crawled in under water, rolled upright and paddled to shore. Another boat was caught on a vertical piton on the drop, and the nose was bent at right angles. The paddler bent the nose back in place over his knee, patched a crack with tape, and went merrily on his way — a great testimony to the toughness of some fiberglass reinforced plastic, not to mention some canoers!

In the next drop, below the bridge, there are vertical steel rods, so be sure to clear this one. About 800 ft. below the bridge surfing waves take you into a small lake. At the foot of the lake is Agers Falls, probably the most spectacular falls to be run in this part of the northeast. One day I saw four boaters, two kayakers, and two canoers in covered boats come down the lake, get out on the right bank and wade out into the water at the top of the falls. They studied the river, the falls, the currents, the rocks and the eddies for a full ten minutes. Then, one by one, they successfully went over the falls in what must have been one of the most exhilarating experiences of their lives. These boaters were real experts. This sort of feat should be tried only by the most experienced boater. On the Port Leyden Quadrangle, three 10-foot contour lines go across the river in a single line, so I would estimate the falls to be about 17 feet high, with another 8-foot drop into the rapids below.

After another half mile you go through a few rifts and come to Shur-form Rapids, a rasp-like rapids where you can chew the bottom right out of your boat.

The climax of this trip is Power Line Rapids, where the river goes under the high voltage line that runs from Marcy to Massena. Here the water drops at the rate of 10 feet in 400 feet, or the equivalent of 132 feet per mile. When the aforementioned boaters reached this point, one of them walked to the foot of the rapids with a throw line in case it was needed for rescue. In this case it wasn't needed, as the boaters came through in good shape with one exception. He broke a paddle in the rocks and was forced to roll over, leave his boat, and tow it to shore.

The road is about 400 feet south of this point over rocky terrain. Crystal Falls is immediately below Power Line Rapids, with its smashing rock pile at the foot of a big cascade. Here the river drops at the rate of 260 feet per mile in a 400-foot stretch, so it is imperative that you take out at Power Line Rapids.

Note: In 1984 a permit was granted to build a dam to generate hydroelectric power here. When completed it will flood Power Line Rapids and Agers Falls.

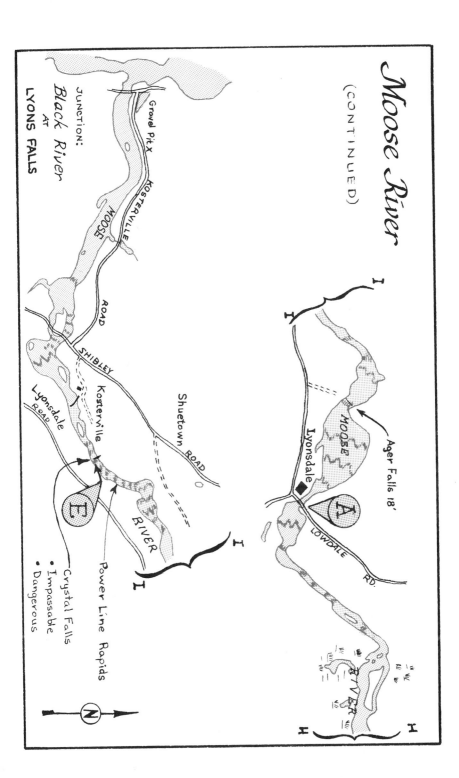

Moose River

(CONTINUED)

JUNCTION:
Black River
AT
LYONS FALLS

Gravel Pit X

KOSTERVILLE

MOOSE

ROAD

SHIBLEY

Kosterville

Shuetown ROAD

Lyonsdale
ROAD

RIVER

• Crystal Falls
• Power Line Rapids

• Dangerous
• Impassable
• Dangerous

E

Ager Falls 18'

MOOSE

Lyonsdale

LOWDALE RD.

RIVER

A

N

NORTH BRANCH

Moose River
North Branch

Tributary: Middle Branch, Moose River

Counties: Herkimer, Hamilton

U.S.G.S. Maps: *Big Moose, Old Forge*

Total Length: 25 mi.

Cruising Length: 16 mi.

Season Recommended: All-season — Lake Rondaxe to Old Forge

Campsites: Nicks Lake Public Campsite

Access	Location	Elev. Feet	Distance Miles	Inter. Dist.	Drop Feet	Gradient Ft./Mile	Rating Class
	Source: Upper Sister Lake	1,930	25		238	10	
A	Big Moose Lake	1,824	16				
				3	67	23	II-III
	Dart Lake	1,757	13				
				2	40	20	II
A	Lake Rondaxe	1,717	11				
				11	25	2	I
A	Jct. Middle Branch at Old Forge	1,692	0				

Big Moose Lake

Big Moose Lake is one of the most unusual lakes in the Adirondacks. It is tucked off the beaten trail by itself and is very irregular in shape, with its North Bay, South Bay, East Bay, and mile-long inlet which could have been called Northeast Bay. It is surrounded by Mt. Tom, Browns Rock and Sugar Loaf and is fed by Upper Sister and Lower Sister lakes. Also feeding into it are Russian Lake and Gull Lake. Terror Lake and Shingle Shanty Pond are nearby. Even the people around Big Moose Lake are different. They seem to feel their corner of the woods is something special. I think they may be justified.

Big Moose Lake was the setting for Theodore Dreiser's novel, *An American Tragedy*, later made into the movie *A Place In the Sun*. It was based on an actual happening, and the locals can show you the location of the murder by drowning which inspired the book.

Moose Lake, elevation 1825 feet, is four miles long and about one mile wide at its widest point. For many years osprey and loons nested in the area. In recent years, however, the use of DDT and acid

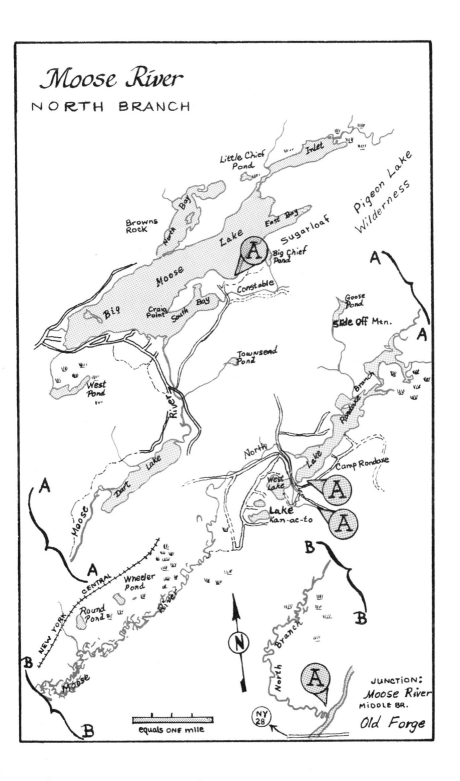

precipitation have been limiting factors in the survival of these birds. They have had to travel farther to pack a lunch to take home to their young. To help overcome this deterioration the residents of Big Moose, when they found a Ph reading of 4.5 in North Bay (a Ph of 7 is neither alkaline nor acid), spread thirty-five tons of lime in the bay. The following year they spread seventy tons and raised the Ph to 5.5. There are many interesting trails into the Pigeon Lake Wilderness Area east of Big Moose Lake. (See Edith Pilcher's "Paddle Hiking Trips in the Pigeon Lake Wilderness," *Adirondac*, July 1983.) There is a public dock at the end of the road on the southwest end of Moose Lake. The eastern end of the lake is bordered by State wilderness land of the Adirondack Forest Preserve.

In the spring when the flow over the dam at the outlet of Big Moose is two to three feet deep, there is a wild ride in store for the adventurous. Both Joe Dunn and Major Bowes of Big Moose have tried it. Joe took the bottom out of a wooden rowboat, and the Major, in a canoe, spilled on the sharp bend part way down the stream. I would not recommend the trip. Two of the hazards of a stream with steep, wooded banks such as this are brush and trees hanging low over the water. Trees, or strainers, all the way across a narrow channel are very bad. A spill will probably carry you down and under the strainer, where your clothing or life jacket may be caught. With the terrific pressure of the current, it is very hard to get loose. Every year, some canoers lose their lives in this manner.

Pinning rocks and blind curves are two other dangers. If you can't see ahead, stop and scout the area before proceeding. A decked boat with a skirt is recommended for trips on rivers of this kind. It not only helps keep the paddler dry but is also easier to maneuver, which helps you beach the boat if necessary.

The drop from Big Moose to Dart Lake is at the rate of 68 feet per one and three tenths mile. This results in fast water. From Dart Lake to Lake Rondaxe there is a straighter run of one and four-tenths miles, with a drop of 37 feet. Dart Lake is about one mile long; Lake Rondaxe about two. A children's summer camp, Adirondack Woodcraft Camp, is located on Lake Rondaxe.

The usual access to the North Branch is from NY 28 to Lake Rondaxe. The North Branch of the Moose looks like the worst scrambled single strand of spaghetti you can imagine. It twists and turns, doubles back and oxbows for miles. It is impossible to measure its length accurately. My best estimate is about eleven miles. To keep in the channel, observe the submerged aquatic plants. The tops of these plants point downstream because they are easily pushed by the current in the main channel. The North Branch of the Moose is a world by itself. You can travel all day and not see another person. Sometimes you share the river only with muskrats, otter, mink and deer. On one trip I saw a fawn on the bank. By a draw stroke I pulled closer. When I was about eight feet away, I got the picture I had hoped for. However, when it heard the snap of the shutter, the fawn rose on all four feet, did an about turn and bounded into the thicket so fast I was astounded. If ever I saw beauty in motion, that was it.

After miles of peaceful paddling, you come to the rapids by the golf course. If the water is high you get a thrilling free ride, but lower water means lining or a portage. The waters open wide in the section above the NY 28 bridge, where you meet the Middle Branch of the Moose. You can paddle up the Middle Branch to Tickner's boat landing, or go below the NY 28 bridge about one-tenth mile to a take-out on the left bank. The section from Lake Rondaxe to the take-out is one of the more tranquil canoe trips in the Adirondacks.

SOUTH BRANCH

Moose River
South Branch

Tributary: Moose River

Counties: Hamilton, Herkimer

U.S.G.S. Maps: 15-minute 1/62500
West Canada Lakes, Old Forge, McKeever

Total Length: 36 mi.

Cruising Length: Indefinite

Season Recommended: May;
Stillwater All-season

Campsites: Nicks Lake Public Campsite
Limekiln Public Campsite
Moose River Recreation Area

Access	Location	Elev. Feet	Distance Miles	Inter. Dist.	Drop Feet	Gradient Ft./Mile	Rating Class
	Source:						
	Little Moose Lake						
	South of Wakely Mt.	2,110	36		602	17	
	Rock Dam	1,805	21				
				11.8	229	20	
	Bisby Road Bridge	1,576	9.2				
				9.2	68	7	
	Jct. of South and						
	Middle Branches	1,508	0				

The South Branch of the Moose River drains a vast area of the southwestern Adirondacks. The easternmost source is "little" Little Moose Lake, elevation 2110′ (not to be confused with "big" Little Moose Lake, elevation 1787′, which is south of First Lake near Old Forge and is the location of the Adirondack League Club). The drainage basin is bounded on the north by the Middle Branch and the Fulton Chain of Lakes; on the east by the Cedar River, which drains into the Hudson; and on the south by West Canada Creek and the Black River.

The South Branch is 36 miles long from its junction with the Middle Branch two miles above McKeever to the headwaters. The drainage area is over 200 square miles and includes most of the 50,000-acre Moose River Recreation Area.

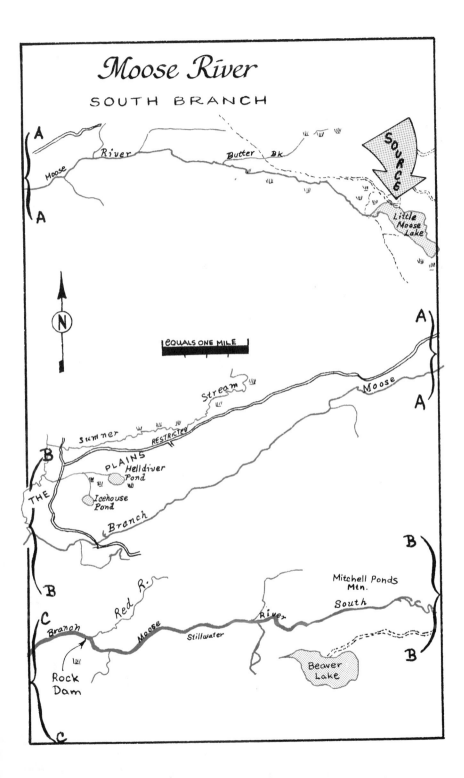

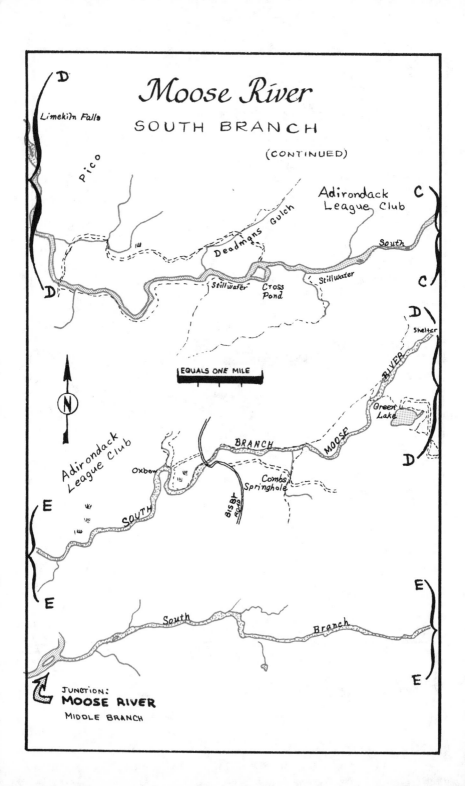

Access to the Recreation Area, coming from the west, is via the Limekiln gate near Limekiln Lake Public Campsite, which is about three miles off NY 28 east of Inlet. Coming from the east, you take the Cedar River Road off NY 28 about one mile west of Indian Lake. Follow up the Cedar River until you come to Wakely Dam on the Cedar River Flow, and you will see the gateway to the recreation area, which is open for hiking, camping, hunting and fishing. For more information contact the Department of Environmental Conservation Regional Headquarters, Ray Brook, New York 12977.

Canoeing is limited to about four miles of the stream, starting at the Beaver Lake Trail junction with the South Branch of the Moose. Most of the trip is flat water, but there are a series of rapids in the middle of the route which are rough in high water. You have to take out at Rock Dam where the Red River joins the South Branch. There is a portage by trail to the Rock Dam Road.

Below the dam is the 100,000 acre property of the Adirondack League Club where canoeing has been prohibited for some time. About twelve miles of the stream flows through club property. The river below the club property would be good canoeing, but access is difficult because of restricted roads. The South Branch is nonetheless important because of its extensive drainage system, which adds a large volume of water to, and makes for great canoeing on, the Moose River proper.

SACANDAGA RIVER

The Indian name Sacandaga means "Cedar in Water" or "Drowned Lands." The Sacandaga, like so many rivers, is divided into three parts, the main river and the east and west branches. Bounded on the north and on the east by the Hudson River system, and on the west by West Canada Creek, it drains a large area of the southern Adirondacks.

The Sacandaga River runs sixty-seven miles, including Great Sacandaga Lake, and empties into the Hudson at Hadley at the rate of 4000 cubic feet per second when the gates are open at Conklinville Dam and Stewart Bridge Dam. It's a terrific river for canoeists.

The West Branch of the Sacandaga starts at Meco Lake, close by the Northville-Lake Placid trail, at an elevation of 2106 feet and about twelve miles south of the village of Lake Pleasant. Its waters flow westerly, southerly, again westerly, then northerly, easterly and again southerly so that the river does a complete circle — a full 360 degrees. The big loop is thirty-one miles long and joins the Sacandaga at the Sacandaga Public Campsite two and one-half miles below Wells on NY 30. The Piseco Lake Outlet joins the West Branch of the Sacandaga about two miles east of NY 10 and two miles north of Shaker Road.

The East Branch starts in the Siamese Ponds Wilderness Area and flows out of Botheration Pond on the east flank of Balm of Gilead Mountain between Thirteenth Lake and Gore Mountain. It drops 1007 feet in its twenty-five mile descent south to NY 8, which it then parallels to its junction with the Sacandaga four miles north of Wells.

SACANDAGA LAKE
LAKE PLEASANT

The main stream starts in Sacandaga Lake, which empties into Lake Pleasant, the outlet of which is the actual start of the Sacandaga River.

Sacandaga River

Tributary: Hudson River

Counties: Hamilton, Warren, Saratoga, Fulton

U.S.G.S. Maps: 15-minute 1/62500
Indian Lake, Thirteenth Lake; Piseco Lake, Lake Pleasant, Harrisburg
7.5-minute 1/24000
Canada Lake, Caroga Lake, Northville; Edinburg, Conklinville, Lake Luzerne

Total Length: 66 mi.

Cruising Length: 55 mi.

Season Recommended: Lakes—All season; Upper River—April-Mid-May; Stewart Bridge Dam Hadley — Spring and releases.

Access	Location	Elev. Feet	Distance Miles	Inter. Dist.	Drop Feet	Gradient Ft./Mile	Rating Class
	Source:						
A	Sacandaga Lake	1,726	66		1,188	18	
A	NY 8 between Sacandaga Lake and Lake Pleasant	1,725	65	1	1	1	I
A	Speculator NY 8 Bridge	1,725	62	3	0		I
A	Kunjamuk Bay	1,725	61	1	0		I
E	Old NY 8 Bridge above Christine Falls	1,720	59	2	5	2	I
A	Jct. NY 8 & NY 10 and Jct. E. Branch	1,093	52				
E	Above dam, Lake Algonguin	982	47	5	111	22	III
A	Below dam, Lake Algonguin at Wells	970	47				
A	Sacandaga Public Campsite and Jct. W. Branch	935	44	3	35	11	II
A	Hope	793	38	6	42	7	II
A	Sacandaga State Launching Site	771	31	7	22	3	I
A	Northampton Beach Public Campsite	771	26	5	0		I
E	Above Conklinville Dam	771	7	19	0		I
A	Below Stewart Bridge Dam	604	3				
E	Jct. Hudson River at Hadley	538	0	3	66	22	III

To canoe Sacandaga Lake and Lake Pleasant you have three choices. The first is to start at the top. Turn north off NY 8 at the west end of the village of Speculator and follow the signs to Moffett's Beach Public Campsite. The launching ramp is on the north edge of the lake; the swimming beach is adjacent to it. The campsite follows along about a mile of shoreline. The rest of the shoreline is mostly uninhabited.

Sacandaga Lake (not to be confused with *Great* Sacandaga Lake) is about two miles in length and the same in width, with a maximum depth of 60 feet. There are fish in the lake, mostly bullheads, yellow perch, walleyes and a few lake trout. The lake is nestled in the hills and surrounded by forests. The outlet and channel to Lake Pleasant is on the southeast shore and well hidden until you get almost to it. Maneuver around the large rocks at the outlet and pick your way gingerly down the channel. There is a one-foot drop between the two lakes which you can usually negotiate in either direction without having to get out and line through. Your second choice is to start at the bottom at the outlet of Lake Pleasant. There is access, with parking, just below the NY 8 bridge at the south edge of Speculator. From here you paddle southwesterly along the north shore about three miles to the outlet of Sacandaga Lake. Go under NY 8 bridge and paddle or pole your way up the half-mile channel to Sacandaga Lake.

The third possibility is to find a good parking spot beside the highway and put your canoe in the channel under the NY 8 bridge west of Speculator and go in the direction you choose, either upstream (north) to Sacandaga Lake or south a very short distance to Lake Pleasant.

Lake Pleasant is about three miles long and a mile wide. You find the same fish here as you do in Sacandaga Lake. Cottages line the north shore, it being adjacent to NY 8, but the south shore is wooded and more primitive, with Speculator Mountain crowning the view to the south.

SPECULATOR TO NORTHVILLE

The canoeable section of the Sacandaga River starts at the outlet of Lake Pleasant on the southeast end of NY 8 in Speculator. Since it is fed by Sacandaga Lake, which feeds into Lake Pleasant, it begins as a canoeable stream and remains so for most of its sixty-two miles. The only exceptions are the rapids from above Christine Falls down through Austin Falls and Auger Falls and the four-mile section of

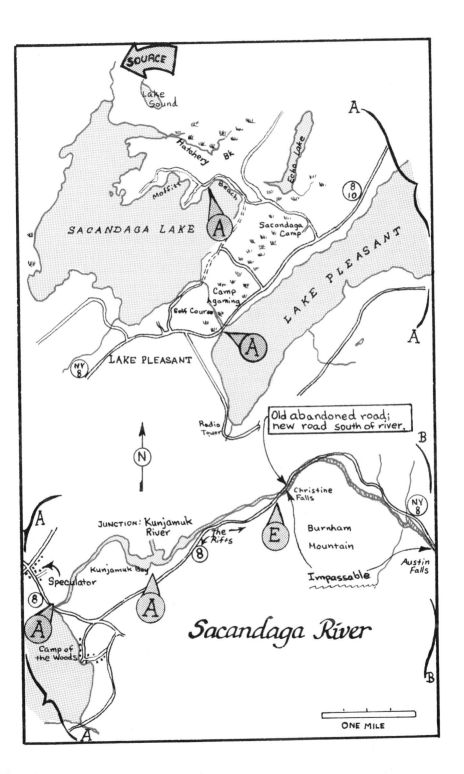

SOURCE

Lake Sound

Hatchery Bk

Echo Lake

8
10

Moffitt

Beach

(A)

SACANDAGA LAKE

Sacandaga
Camp

LAKE PLEASANT

Camp
Agaming

Golf Course

(A)

LAKE PLEASANT

NY
8

A

A

Radio
Tower

Old abandoned road;
new road south of river.

N

B

Christine
Falls

NY
8

A

JUNCTION: Kunjamuk
River

The
Rifts

(E)

Burnham

Mountain

Speculator

Kunjamuk Bay

8

Austin
Falls

8

(A)

Impassable

A

Camp of
the Woods

Sacandaga River

B

ONE MILE

A

Stewart Bridge Reservoir on the lower Sacandaga. There is access with good parking just below the NY 8 bridge in Speculator on the left bank.

The first four miles of the river are stillwater and a sheer delight. It can be paddled all summer long since it is a deep water channel until you get to the rapids above the old NY 8 bridge four miles down the stream. The river is overhung with lovely trees, and there are flowering shrubs and flowers on the banks.

At some places the stream widens, as at Kunjamuk Bay, one and six-tenths miles from the start. Here there is parking off NY 8 at State Marker No. 1296. For a trip description see **Kunjamuk River.**

Below Kunjamuk Bay the river winds and turns through forest glades. You can take your canoe out of the river before you come to the rapids just above the old NY 8 bridge, which turns off present NY 8 (Route 30) at State Marker 1309. This section is very dangerous, suitable only for experts. Each steep drop must be scouted, for this is a narrow, constricted, gorge-like passage punctuated with impassable falls at Christine, Austin, and Auger falls. *Class IV-VI Water.*

Parts of the next six miles may be canoed, but to get the most out of your trip I would suggest you skip it, unless you want to run one-half mile, portage one-quarter mile, run one-quarter mile and then portage two miles. Otherwise, put your canoe back in the river at the junction of NY 8 and NY 30 at State Marker 1376. Go across the bridge from NY 30 and put in on the left bank below the bridge.

The next four miles down to Algonquin Lake at Wells drops one hundred and eleven feet and has some good Class III water when the river is running medium high to high, approaching Class IV at high water. This is an exciting race. Though you have NY 30 on the right bank and Hamilton County Route 8 on the left, you are down in the trough with boulders to dodge and are totally unaware of the roads on either side of you. This stretch can be scouted from old Rte. 8 on the east side of the river.

NY 30 crosses the river above Lake Algonquin, and you can take out here or paddle another mile and one-half and take out on the right bank of Lake Algonquin just above the dam, which is within sight of NY 30 just across the bridge in the hamlet of Wells.

There is parking and good access just below the dam on the right bank. Put in on the right bank of the river just below the dam, which is just west of NY 30 in the village of Wells and which backs up the water for about one and three-quarters miles.

As you go under the first bridge and through a couple of chutes, your canoe picks up speed. A drop of 47 feet in the next two and a half miles

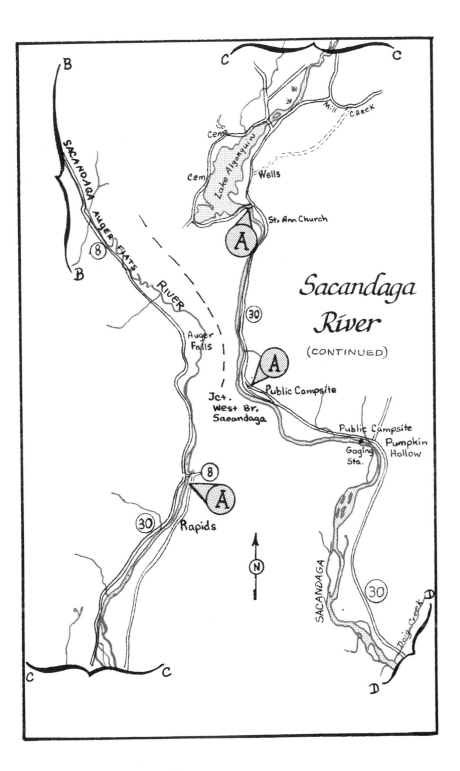

B

SACANDAGA AUGER FLATS RIVER

(8)

B

Cem

Cem

Lake Algonquin

Wells

Mill Creek

C

C

St. Ann Church

A

(30)

Sacandaga River

(CONTINUED)

Auger Falls

A

Public Campsite

Jct.
West Br.
Sacandaga

Public Campsite

Pumpkin Hollow

Gaging Sta.

(8)

A

(30)

Rapids

(N)

SACANDAGA

(30)

Doig Creek

C

C

D

D

down to the Sacandaga Public Campsite and the junction of the West Branch makes for a spirited Class II run. You can do it in half an hour. A fast chute around to the right deposits your canoe in a pool above another dam at the campsite. During the summer months splash boards are put up to form a swimming pool. At other times, with medium high water, you can run the dam, but be sure the water level is high enough so you can make it through without damaging your canoe. When the water is low the stern thuds on the lower end of the apron.

The Sacandaga Public Campsite, with large white pines and a carpet of pine needles, was opened early in 1983 as a pilot project to accommodate canoers and other outdoorsmen. When I was there on May 13, 1983, there were pit toilets, no running water, and no caretaker. Payment was on the honor system. When we went back on May 15th, however, the water was on. With proper cooperation from early campers, perhaps this program will be extended both here and at other facilities to benefit not only summer visitors but also canoers in the spring and hunters in the fall.

There is almost continuous fast water for about three miles below the campsite. The drop is about 30 feet per mile, and it is a lively Class II+-III run with crisscrossing currents and good-sized standing waves and haystacks. The heavy water stretch ends at the big curve just south of the gauging station. A good egress is at the Town Hall of Hope where the river comes alongside NY 30 and where the bank up which you drag your canoe is not too steep.

If you wish to continue, there is an access at the NY 30 bridge and another good one at the State Launching Site at Northville, adjacent to NY 30. This trip can easily be combined with a trip on the West Branch. Following the section of the river just described is 32-mile long Great Sacandaga Lake, which was formed by the building of the Conklinville Dam.

GREAT SACANDAGA LAKE

From the State Launching Site at Northville on the Sacandaga you have two choices. One is to go to the lower Sacandaga River which is below Stewart Dam. The other is to canoe thirty-two-mile-long Great Sacandaga Lake. With its 125 miles of shoreline, there is plenty to explore. The lake, which has a maximum depth of seventy feet, covers 26,700 acres. It is noted for its big fish, the record being a forty-six-

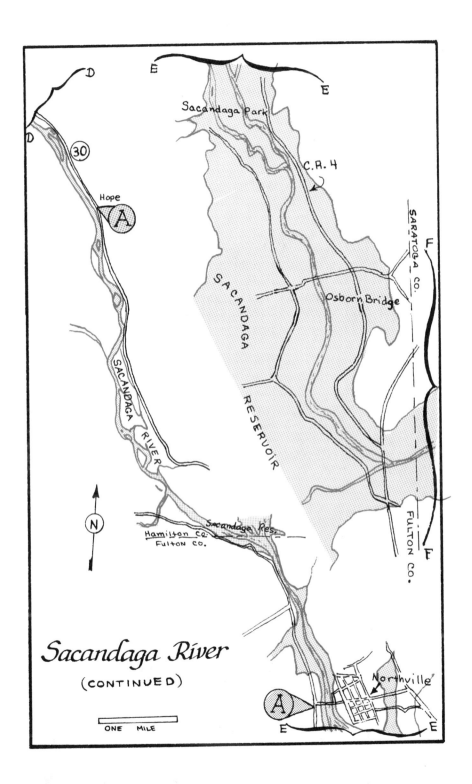

D

E

E

Sacandaga Park

C.R. 4

30

Hope

(A)

SARATOGA CO.

F

Osborn Bridge

SACANDAGA

F

SACANDAGA RESERVOIR

SACANDAGA RIVER

FULTON CO.

N

Sacandaga Res.

Hamilton Co.
Fulton Co.

Sacandaga River

(CONTINUED)

ONE MILE

(A)

Northville

E

E

pound northern pike. In addition to pike, it has walleyes, bass, yellow perch and other fish. Be sure to keep a weather eye out. This lake can develop strong winds and whitecaps and has claimed the life of more than one canoer.

Northville is across the bridge from NY 30. This village's claim to fame is its birds. As Capistrano has its swallows, and Hinkley, Ohio its buzzards, Northville has its chimney swifts. For the last sixty years, at 8:00 p.m. on May 6th, a colony of these darting birds has appeared in Northville, where they spiral around an abandoned factory chimney and then, following their leader, swoop down into the dark chimney. There they find nests and start another generation of swifts.

Four miles on down the right shore of the lake you find North-hampton Beach Public Campsite. This 224-unit campsite has a nice swimming beach and a launching area. In fact, there are launching areas at most of the villages around the lake. Be sure to secure permission if beaching on private property.

The lake shore is controlled by the Hudson River-Black River Regulating District, which supervises the flow at the Conklinville and Stewart Dams at the foot of the lake. There is a take-out on the right bank just above the Conklinville Dam near Conklinville. From here you have to portage to below the Stewart Road Dam, as canoeing is not allowed between the two dams. The gate is open on the north end of Stewart Road, which goes over the dam, throughout the summer when the commercial rafters are running — usually six days a week. It would be well to call the Hudson River Rafting Company to verify the schedule.

You can drive down to the left bank of the river to put in. Be careful of the surge from the release at the dam. The Niagara-Mohawk Corporation has a high fence around the launching site below the dam. However, several rafting companies do have access to this site, so if your arrival coincided with theirs (weekdays 9 a.m. to 5 p.m.; call Pat Cunningham at 518-251-3215 to make sure they will be running on the day you plan to be there) I believe you could put in just below the dam. Otherwise, go up the Sacandaga River on the road from Hadley Luzerne on the north side, or left bank, and turn left onto the old Stewart Bridge Road, which dead-ends at a barricade about 150 feet from the river. Be sure to park away from the barricade.

The release from the dam is governed by the demand for electricity. Normally, they release water from the dam five days a week all through the season. When we were there the water level dropped during the period from 11:50 a.m. to 1 p.m., but it might be well to call ahead to

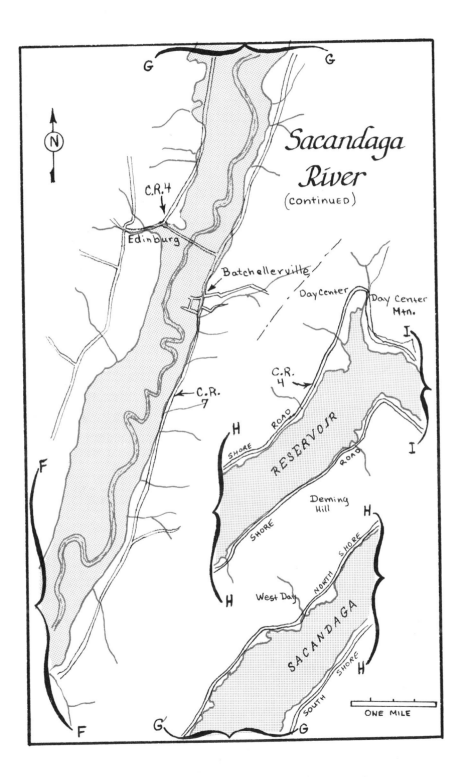

N

G   G

Sacandaga
River
(CONTINUED)

C.R.4

Edinburg

Batchellerville

Day Center

Day Center
Mtn.

I

C.R.
4

H   SHORE   ROAD   RESERVOIR   I

C.R.
7

ROAD

Deming
Hill   H

F   SHORE

NORTH SHORE   H

H   West Day

SACANDAGA

H

SOUTH SHORE

ONE MILE

F   G   G

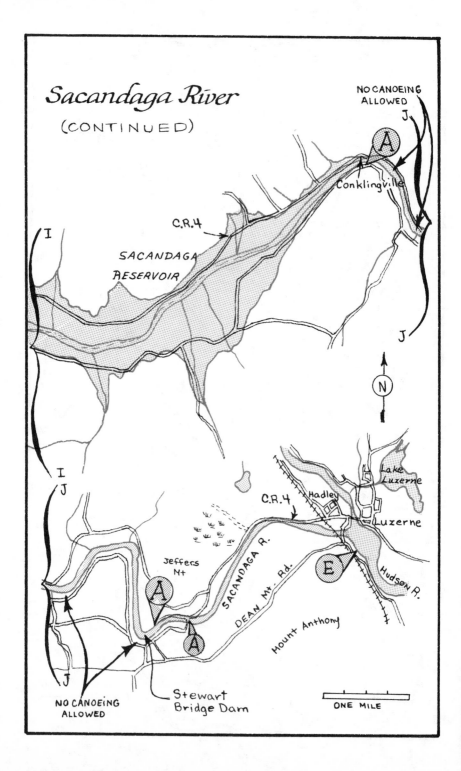

Sacandaga River
(CONTINUED)

NO CANOEING ALLOWED

J

A

Conklingville

C.R.4

SACANDAGA RESERVOIR

I

J

N

I

J

C.R.4

Hadley

Lake Luzerne

Luzerne

Jeffers Nt

SACANDAGA R.

DEAN Mt. Rd.

E

Hudson R.

Mount Anthony

A

A

Stewart Bridge Dam

NO CANOEING ALLOWED

J

ONE MILE

find out release times. On the day we went down, the low water reading was two and five-tenths feet; the high four and five-tenths feet.

From just below the dam there are some nice Class II-III rapids before you come to an eddy about a mile long. There is a gauging station on the left bank. A little below this the river gradient becomes steeper, and you encounter several exciting rapids. With the release most of the boulders are covered; however, there can be quite high haystacks. In the vicinity of the road and railroad bridges the rapids approach Class III when the water level is high. With the fast current the trip is over in about half an hour, much too short a time for such an exhilarating ride.

As the fast waters of the Sacandaga meet the slower waters of the Hudson, interesting whirlpools and boils develop. If you are a novice, this may startle you. Paddle over to the rocks on the left bank of the Hudson for a close-up look at impressive Hadley Luzerne Falls.

You take out on the left bank of the Sacandaga at its junction with the Hudson. The trip down the Sacandaga is short but good, especially in summer when the water temperature is up and the river and scenery are most enjoyable.

EAST BRANCH

The East Branch of the Sacandaga River is a sleeper. If the flow of this river could be stabilized so that the excess water over a normal flow—say 200 cubic feet per second—from January through April could be held and released in June, July and August, it could be a great summer recreation area for canoers, campers, fishermen and picnickers. All of the resources are there.

The optimum place to start canoeing on the East Branch is at NY State Marker 1056 about one mile northeast of the former hamlet of Oregon. Here the stream elevation is 1400 feet. For the next ten miles the stream drops gently, about 140 feet. Then you come to impassable Griffins Falls, a rocky gorge dropping about 20 feet in 200. You could carry around the falls, but it is very rough; you probably will want to leave a shuttle car across the bridge and up the stream a short distance within sight of the river. To reach this point, turn left (north) off NY 8 going east at State Marker 1260 onto a gravel road.

Take out on the right bank at the settlement of Griffin, about 200 feet above the bridge. (Though today it is hard to believe, Griffin was once a thriving tannery town with a reputed 252 houses.) Load the canoe on

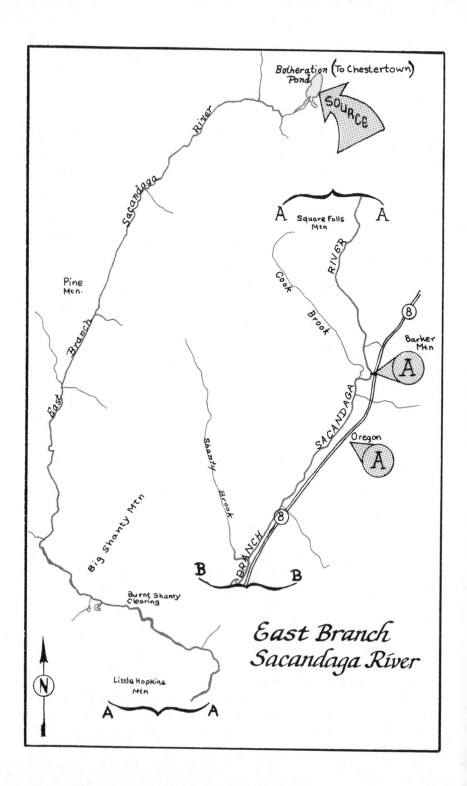

Botheration Pond (To Chestertown)

SOURCE

Sacandaga River

A   Square Falls Mtn   A

Cook Brook

RIVER

(8)

Barker Mtn

A

Oregon

A

SACANDAGA

Pine Mtn.

East Branch

Shanty Brook

Big Shanty Mtn

(8)

BRANCH

B   B

Burnt Shanty Clearing

N

Little Hopkins Mtn

A   A

East Branch
Sacandaga River

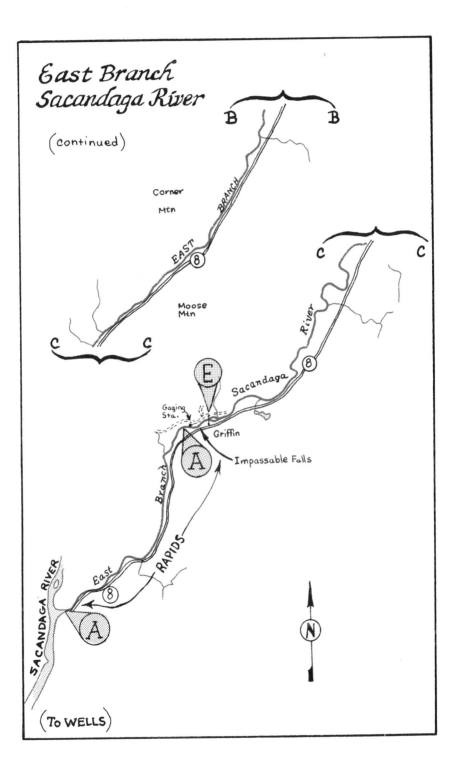

Sacandaga River
East Branch

Tributary: Sacandaga River

Counties: Hamilton, Warren

U.S.G.S. Maps: 15-minute 1/62500
Lake Pleasant, Harrisburg, Thirteenth Lake

Total Length: 25 mi.

Cruising Length: 12 mi.

Season Recommended: April-Mid-May

Campsite: Sacandaga Public Campsite

Access	Location	Elev. Feet	Distance Miles	Inter. Dist.	Drop Feet	Gradient Ft./Mile	Rating Class
	Botheration Pond Balm of Gilead Mt.	2,100	25		1,021	41	
A	Stream nearest NY 8	1,400	12				
				.8	20	25	II
A	Oregon	1,380	11.2				
				8.4	120	14	II
A	Griffin	1,260	2.8				
				2.8	167	60	III
A	Jct. Sacandaga River at Jct. of NY 8 and NY 30	1,093	0				

the car and drive out to NY 8. If you do decide to carry, just below the bridge at Griffin Falls is a beautiful spot for a picnic.

A word of caution is in order about the next two and eight-tenths miles down to the junction of the Sacandaga. The river changes from a pussycat to a roaring lion. It is one continuous, steep rock garden filled with boulders, and you must have high water to get through it. When it is high you have Class III-plus water, going to Class IV water when the river runs above six feet. In this two and eight-tenths miles the river drops 167 feet, or over sixty feet per mile. One half-mile section has a gradient of 100 feet per mile. Paddling in this kind of water in a thirty-pound boat is more exciting than any roller coaster ride in the world.

WEST BRANCH

The West Branch of the Sacandaga River starts in Meco Lake and adjacent swamps. The Northville-Lake Placid trail skirts the west edge of the lake.

Canoeing begins at the bridge on the north edge of Arietta on NY 10, which is about twelve miles south of the junction of NY 10 and NY 8

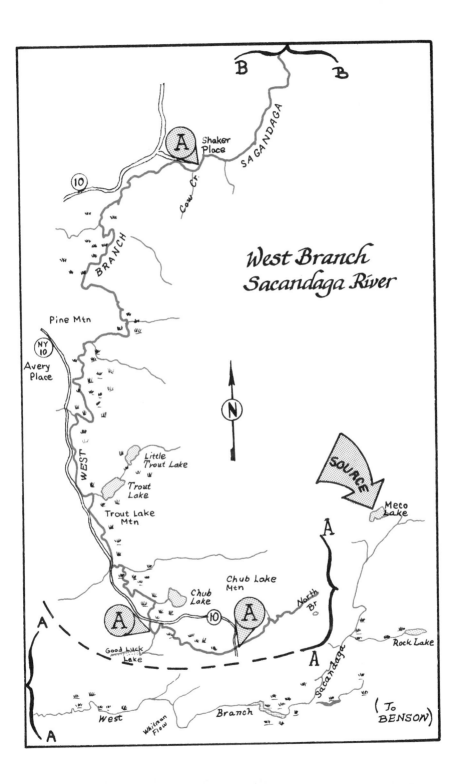

B B

A Shaker Place

SACANDAGA

10

West Branch
Sacandaga River

COW CR.

BRANCH

Pine Mtn

NY 10

Avery Place

N

WEST

Little Trout Lake

Trout Lake

Trout Lake Mtn

SOURCE

Meco Lake

A

Chub Lake Mtn

Chub Lake

10

A

North Br

A

Rock Lake

A

Good Luck Lake

A

Sacandaga

West

Whitman Flow

Branch

(To BENSON)

A

on the south edge of Piseco Lake. From this access it is a mile down to the next bridge on NY 10, where camping is allowed. It is possible to pull a small camp trailer in on either bank of the stream, and there is easy access to the river. In the next seven and four-tenths miles the river drops seventeen feet. While there is some current all the way, the water is deep and can be canoed all summer in either direction. About three miles downriver there is a beaver dam which has been in the stream for many years. One-quarter of a mile below the bridge you can paddle back into Chubb Lake on the right. Another mile and a half farther down you can go into Trout Lake, also on the right. When we were there in September 1983, we met some people who had seen a golden eagle earlier in the day.

Sacandaga River
West Branch

Tributary: Sacandaga River

County: Hamilton

U.S.G.S. Maps: 15-minute 1/62500
Piseco Lake, Lake Pleasant

Total Length: 32 mi.

Cruising Length: Upper 8.4, lower 8 mi.

Season Recommended: Lower Section —
April-May; Arietta-Shaker Place, all season.

Campsites: Sacandaga Public Campsite,
Little Sand Point Public Campsite

Access	Location	Elev. Feet	Distance Miles	Inter. Dist.	Drop Feet	Gradient Ft./Mile	Rating Class
	Source: Meco Lake on Northville-Placid Trail	2,106	32		1,174	37	
A	NY 10 Bridge at North edge of Arietta	1,660	24.4				
				1	3	3	I
A	Lower NY 10 Bridge	1,657	23.4				
				3.4	7	2	I
	Avery Place	1,650	20				
				4	10	2.5	I
E	Shaker Place	1,640	16				
				3	32	10	II
	Piseco Lake Outlet *(Impassable)*	1,608	13				
				5	338	68	VI
A	Whitehouse	1,270	8				
				6.3	245	39	II-III
A	Black Bridge	1,025	1.7				
				1.7	93	55	II-III
E	Jct. Sacandaga R.	932	0				

The stream meanders across the fen, with sweet gale, red-stemmed dogwood and elderberry on the banks. In September the most striking flower is the Canadian burnet with its spike-like white flower standing above the marsh grasses. You will also see an occasional cardinal flower along the edges of the stream. Near Avery Place, with its large white hotel, the river comes near the road, but there is no easy access. The river then goes east around Pine Mountain. After a minimum of two hours of paddling, the trip ends at Shaker Place, a large gravel borrow pit about two-tenths of a mile off NY 10 at State Marker 1090.

Because of the deep channel, you can canoe the West Branch of the Sacandaga on through autumn, when the fall colors make it a most pleasurable trip.

Piseco Lake

Piseco Lake is an integral part of the drainage system of the West Branch of the Sacandaga River. It is a very popular spot in the lower Adirondacks with three State public campsites, all on the northwest shore: Poplar Point, Little Sand Point and Point Comfort. To reach it go east from Utica on NY 8 and turn off NY 8 on County Road 24 to Piseco. You can see all three campsites along the lake shore. If you are going west, just reverse the process by going to Piseco first. The lake is about five miles long and a little more than a mile wide. It has a maximum depth of 129 feet. It contains lake trout, brook trout, landlocked salmon, bass and perch.

Besides exploring along the shores by canoe, you can go down the bay at the southwest corner. After going southerly about a mile you turn east into two-mile-long Big Bay, the east end of which terminates at a dam just below NY 10. Carry around the dam on the left bank.

If you prefer, you can come by car on NY 10 to the dam for an interesting trip up to Spy Lake. Travel eastward down the outlet for eight-tenths of a mile to where the outlet turns south. Spy Lake Outlet, a small stream, comes in on the left. Follow up the outlet another eight-tenths of a mile to one and one-half mile long Spy Lake, a little gem nestled in the woods. There are a few cottages on the north shore, but with the Silver Lake Wilderness Area around most of the lake there are plenty of choice camping and picnicking spots on the rest of the shore.

Piseco Outlet goes on south about two miles, where it joins the West Branch of the Sacandaga River. It is possible to paddle this section and then go up the West Branch to Shaker Place, but since the river drops 32 feet from Shaker Place to the Piseco Lake Outlet it would be quite a workout, though interesting.

Below Piseco Lake Outlet and the junction of the West Branch you are in a no man's land as far as the river is concerned. My advice is to forget it. It drops at the rate of 68 feet per mile for five miles with most of the drop in the short distance between Big Eddy to a point below Owl Pond Outlet, where the river drops 180 feet in a mile and two-tenths—a gradient of 150 feet per mile. There are two impassable falls in the gorge.

Lower West Branch

The Lower West Branch of the Sacandaga River is one of the most challenging and exciting small streams in the Adirondacks. When I was there on May 13, 1983 the stream was running at medium level, and we scraped going through a few of the rapids. Two weeks earlier the level was about one and one-half feet higher—a good level for canoeing.

To reach the West Branch of the Sacandaga turn off NY 30 at the lower end of Wells onto County Road 5. Cross the bridge just below the dam which forms Lake Algonquin and go about three-quarters of a mile; then turn left on the West River Road. Go about two miles to Black Bridge Road, where you will see the West Branch. Keep on the north side (left bank) of the stream. You may need a four-wheel-drive vehicle if the road is very muddy or has washouts. When we were there in 1983 we made it, albeit slowly, in a two-wheel-drive Datsun.

About six miles beyond the bridge the road ends in a *cul de sac*. You will see the remains of a chimney from an old hotel. This is just below the suspension bridge over which passes the Northville-Lake Placid trail. Carry your gear down to the stretch of calm water below the bridge.

About 100 yards down the stream you turn right and suddenly drop down into a souse hole; you then continue on through some gentle rapids. From here on you are busy reading the river all the way. The roughest water is about three and one-half miles downstream from the start. This is a Class II rapid, reaching Class III at high water levels. Watch out for the remains of an old log dam just above Jiminy Creek where the log base is still in the river. In this area the stream reaches a gradient of 66 feet per mile.

From Black Bridge to the junction of the Sacandaga the gradient is 55 feet per mile, qualifying the river as one of the steepest runnable passages in the state. If you catch this stream at the right level you will never forget it.

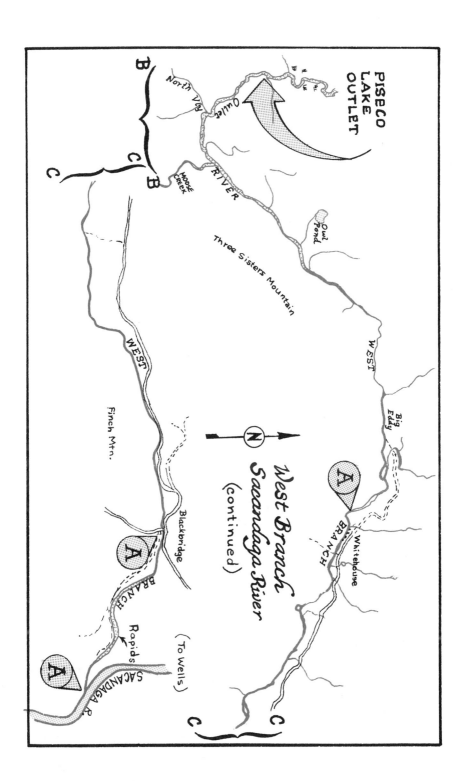

Fall Stream and Vly Lake

The Sacandaga River system has a great variety of waters. Two examples are Fall Stream and Vly Lake. Fall Stream flows into Piseco Lake on its northeastern border directly south of the hamlet of Piseco. You can line up the stream for a quarter of a mile from the lake to the bridge through light rapids, but the easier approach is to bring your canoe by car 1.6 miles from NY 8 toward the hamlet of Piseco and put in on the right (north) bank just above the bridge where there is stillwater. This is private property. Be sure to respect others' rights and do not block the road or the path by the stream.

This access is about .4 mile from the Northville-Placid trail if you are coming from the State public campsite on the northwest shore of Piseco Lake-Little Sand Point and Point Comfort. Poplar Point is now primarily a day use site.

Fall Stream above the highway bridge is stillwater a few hundred feet above Fall Lake. One beautiful June day, with mosquitoes stabbing us in the back, it took us only twenty minutes to reach Fall Lake, a pretty little body of water about .3 mile long and .1 mile wide. Going up the inlet you come to a small beaver dam, and you begin to see evidence of the beavers' foraging — chewed ends of tag alder which they have not yet stored away. We surprised one of the animals, and it immediately disappeared under water.

The banks are covered with bunchberry *(Cornus canadensis)*, the lowest-growing of the dogwoods, and American Mountain ash. Wild raisin and *Viburnum* bloom in season. Tall spires of balsam fir also line the banks. On higher, dryer ground the red spruce in Spring 1984 were heavily loaded with cones. Many theories about the reason for this abundance of cones have been postulated, such as a hard winter ahead, or the trees going into a decline. Since I do not think that groves of trees prognosticate, my theory is simply that we had a very wet spring which caused an exceptionally heavy seed crop.

A short distance above the first beaver dam the stream narrows, and you cross several more dams. Two miles above Fall Lake you come to Vly Lake, which is overshadowed on the east by the steep slopes of Vly Lake Mountain, ascending 2052 feet above sea level. Starting one-fourth mile above the put-in, you enter the Wild Forest land of the Adirondack Forest Preserve. This is State of New York land, so camping is permitted. Above Vly Lake, Fall Stream continues on into the wilderness approximately nine miles.

Piseco Lake Outlet and Spy Lake

Piseco Lake outlet flows out of the eastern end of Big Bay, which is south of the western end and part of Piseco Lake. It begins at a dam just below the bridge on NY 10, State Marker 1135, which is 1.3 miles south of NY 8. You can paddle from the State campsites on Piseco Lake southwest, then south into Big Bay and east to the bridge, carrying left around the dam and dumping your canoe into the outlet. An easier way is to drive to the bridge to unload your canoe. Don't block the road on the left bank; there is ample parking nearby on the right bank (1984). When we did the trip and put in on the right bank, we scraped over rocks getting into the stillwater. Upon our return we found that splash boards had been added to the dam, and the channel we had gone down was almost dry. Be sure to check this out or portage down a road 600 feet on the left bank to the access at stillwater.

You travel .8 mile westward in an ever-widening trough to where the Spy Lake outlet enters on the left, or north, edge of the stream. At this point the outlet turns abruptly south. After .2 mile, Mud Lake outlet comes in on the left. Another .5 mile south rapids suddenly appear, and hardwood and mixed forest starts. If the water is medium-high you have an exciting ride dodging rocks for 100 yards; you then come to a six-foot drop that would be almost impossible to negotiate without smashing your canoe, but just before you come to the rapids there is a dock on the right bank and a portage up the hill to the cabin of the Outlet Club. You then go down the hill to the stream below the aforementioned six-foot drop.

Before leaving the stillwater, determine if you really want to go any farther by canoe. It is about 2.5 miles to the junction of the West Branch of the Sacandaga, with a drop of 42 feet. Below the junction is *impassable* rapids and falls.

From the junction up the West Branch to Shaker Place is three miles with a rise of 32 feet. Either way you travel it is a hard day's work and probably not worth the effort. Of course you can always bushwhack, but that's a tough way to canoe.

Spy Lake outlet (mentioned above) may be a little difficult to find, but by checking the north, or left, bank at the bend carefully, you will discover the small stream which small beaver dams keep passable most of the year. During the dry summer months you may have to line up the stream for short distances. It is .6 mile up to the lake. Be sure to locate and position the outlet bay as you enter the lake, since the outlet is hidden from the lake proper. Private property with buildings can be seen on the western shore, but more than three-quarters of the shoreline is in the Wilderness category of the Adirondack Forest Preserve.

Near the northern shore is a small island excellent for a picnic or for camping. It is high and dry with good swimming along the shore. I call it Five Pines Island because it has five large nice white pines on it. There is room for about six tents, but there is one drawback: the island is hardly big enough for a pit privy. However, it is only about 200 feet to the mainland where one could be dug well back from the shore. There are other camping possibilities farther east along the shore of the lake. Spy Lake is one of the many delightful little lakes which dot the Adirondacks and are seldom visited. Especially off-season, you may consider them your very own.

Heading back to the outlet we played hide-and-seek with a white-tailed doe that had ventured out into the lake to an island of growing reeds. After about ten minutes she decided to take to the cover of the hardwood forest. Rounding another curve on the outlet we came to within fifteen feet of an American bittern. Startled, the bird stretched for the sky and awkwardly took off for less crowded territory. Returning back up the outlet, we felt that the day had been well spent.

SALMON RIVER

Salmon River

Tributary: Lake Ontario

Counties: Oswego, Lewis

U.S.G.S. Maps: 7.5-minute 1/24000
Pulaski, Richland, Orwell, Redfield

Total Length: 48 mi.

Cruising Length: 13 (Salmon Reservoir 6)

Season Recommended: All seasons with
releases (Call 315-298-6531)

Campsites: Selkirk Shores State Park

Access	Location	Elev. Feet	Distance Miles	Inter. Dist.	Drop Feet	Gradient Ft./Mile	Rating Class
	Source: East of Little John Game Management Area	1,740	48		1,494	31	
A	Altmar	518	13				
				9	218	24	III
A	Pulaski	300	4				
				4	54	14	I-III
A	Lake Ontario	246	0				

The playful Salmon River has the potential of becoming a summer long recreation area for canoers and kayakers because of the Salmon River Reservoir near Redford operated by the Niagara-Mohawk Corporation. Its hydroelectric station is powered by releases from the reservoir during times of extra demand for power from Syracuse and vicinity (normally the middle of the day during the week), and the

Pulaski Chamber of Commerce, working with canoeing groups, has been able to get releases on weekends about three times during the summer. If these weekend releases could be doubled in frequency, with set dates such as the first and third weekends in June, July and August, it would be a great service to the canoeing public.

The Salmon River starts on the Tug Hill Plateau, one of the most unusual land forms in New York State. The Tug Hill region is about fifty miles long north and south, and thirty miles wide east to west. It is bounded on the north and east by the Black River, on the west (approximately) by Interstate 81, and on the south by Oneida Lake.

The slope on the west side, starting at Lake Ontario (elevation of 246 feet), rises to approximately 1900 feet. When the westerly winds blow across warm Lake Ontario, they pick up water vapor. As the moisture laden air goes up the slope it is cooled, and the moisture condenses and falls as rain or snow on the plateau. This accounts for the heavy snowfalls in the Tug Hill area, once in recent years reaching 400 inches with four feet falling on Barnes Corners in one twenty-four-hour period.

The flat terrain covered with trees and swamps acts like a giant sponge, and the water is released gradually down the rivers. (The stream flow could be stabilized much more than it is at present by applying all of the conservation measures available plus some new ideas: strip cropping, contour planting, and reforestation on terraces which would fit the topography.)

The U.S.G.S. maps show many marshy areas where low-cost water impoundments ranging from a few acres to hundreds of acres could be made without hurting the environment. These activities could provide employment and stabilize the wood using industry in the area. The resulting even stream flow would benefit the canoer, the power companies, fishermen, hunters and farmers.

Access to the Salmon River is on the left bank above the bridge in Altmar which is just off NY 13 east of Pulaski. There is limited parking and a ramp to the stream which should not be blocked.

The usual trip from Altmar to the Black Hole below the lower bridge in Pulaski is about nine miles. Another three miles will take you to Port Ontario on NY 3, with a take-out at the Pine Grove in Selkirk Shores State Park on the left bank just below. During a release the water flows briskly for two and one-half miles down to Pineville Bridge, where there is a parking and access area operated by the New York State Department of Environmental Conservation (DEC). This stream is used primarily by fishermen, so treat them well and give them a wide berth.

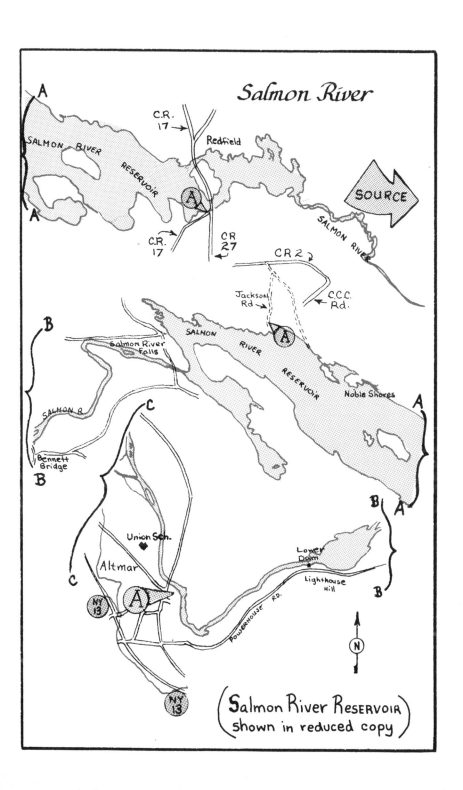

The river starts dropping and the chutes get more interesting (Class II) in the next three miles down to the County Road 2A bridge. Here, on the right bank adjacent to the landfill operation, is a large parking area and a paved ramp down to the stream. A long fast rapid follows down to Interstate 81. Below are several fast Class III rapids. The heaviest whitewater is as you approach the NY 11 bridge in the village of Pulaski. By maneuvering, you can avoid some of the haystacks, but the roller coaster effect of the high waves is exhilarating and fun. With an open boat you are apt to take on some water unless you back paddle hard and ride up and over the waves. Even then, you probably cannot avoid taking on some water as you plunge into the next souse hole. That is one of the joys of closed boats: You can charge through and come out dry except for the area above your spray skirt.

At the next curve the water slaps against a cliff on the left, causing some violent cross currents and haystacks. The water continues challenging right on down to the Black Hole, where you take out on the right bank just below the treatment plant. Just above the Black Hole is a large municipal parking lot, reached from Lake Street. If the gates are open, you can drive down close to the stream to pick up your boat.

If you want to extend your trip three miles, go down below Port Ontario, which is on NY 3, to Selkirk Shores State Park on the left bank. You can drive to the Pine Grove take-out area by turning right before going through the gate (where there is a charge for entering the State Park).

The Salmon River was full of salmon in the early days and now, after many years, again teems with Chinook and Coho salmon and steelhead trout. New York State has recently completed a fish hatchery above Altmar which is open to visitors. Here millions of salmonoids are raised and released in the Great Lakes fishery each year.

The Salmon is truly one of the great recreation rivers of the state. It is gentle at first, then increases to a crescendo of moderate rapids and ends in a climax of Class III water that is fun yet not unusually dangerous. To find out the time of releases from the Niagara-Mohawk impoundment call 315-298-6531. This information is given out one day at a time.

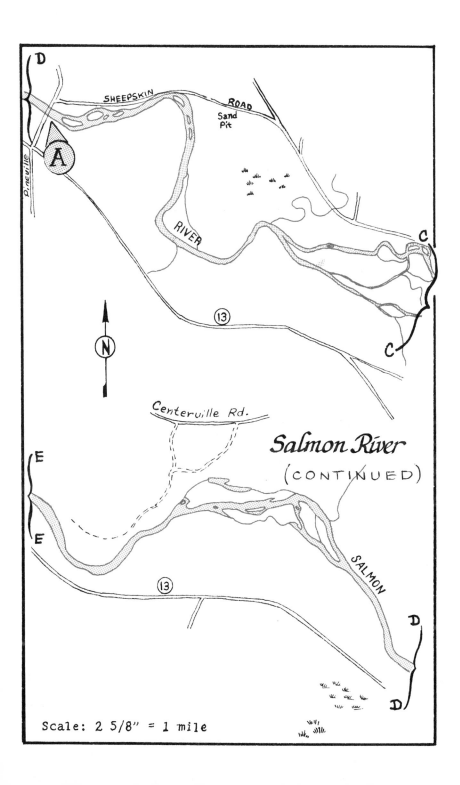

D

SHEEPSKIN ROAD
Sand Pit

Pineville

A

RIVER

C

C

N

13

Centerville Rd.

Salmon River

(CONTINUED)

E

E

SALMON

13

D

D

Scale: 2 5/8" = 1 mile

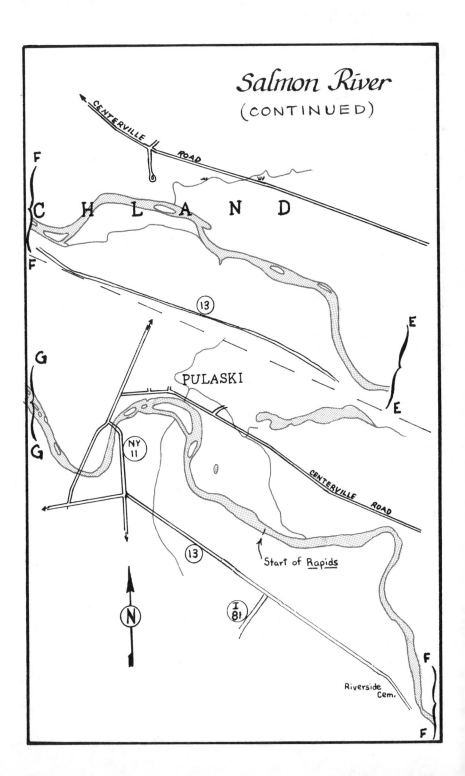

Salmon River
(CONTINUED)

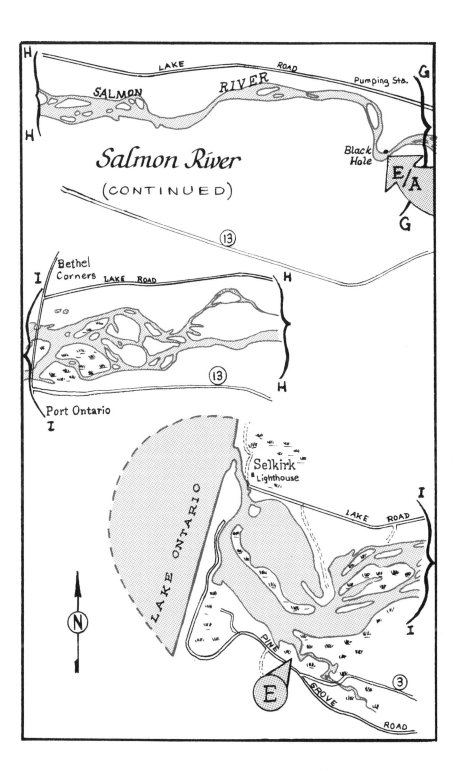

H H LAKE ROAD G

SALMON RIVER Pumping Sta.

Salmon River

(CONTINUED)

Black Hole

E/A

G

⑬

Bethel Corners LAKE ROAD H

I

⑬ H

Port Ontario

I

Selkirk
Lighthouse

I

LAKE ROAD

LAKE ONTARIO

I

N

PINE

E

GROVE

③

ROAD

SALMON RIVER RESERVOIR

The Salmon River Reservoir provides all-season (ice-out to ice-in) canoeing. This pretty, six-mile-long body of water with access at either end offers the flat water canoer a number of possibilities.

You can start at the west end of the lake by putting in at the end of Jackson Road off County Road 2 just east of Stillwater, or you can start at the east end by putting in at the south end of NY 285 bridge near Redfield. The islands and beaches along the way provide excellent picnicking and swimming. There is a large block of State land along the north shore by the C.C.C. road which is open to the public.

SCHROON RIVER

The Schroon River is one of the most delightful and amiable streams in the eastern Adirondacks. It murmurs to the novice paddler, gurgles to the intermediate, and extends a tantalizing invitation to the advanced whitewater enthusiast. In the fifty-seven miles from Sharp Bridge Campsite south of Elizabethtown to the junction of the Hudson River at Thurman Station about three miles west of Warrensburg, the canoeist encounters all degrees of difficulty, from Class I (still water, little current) to Class III (difficult, high turbulence). Fourteen miles down its course, the stream is interrupted by eight-mile-long Schroon Lake, famous as a summer recreation area. Its wooded shores on the east and magnificent view of the Adirondack Mountains to the west entrance all who visit it.

Accessibility to the Schroon River is exceptionally good. Interstate 87 (the Northway) and U.S. Highway 9 run parallel to it, while three New York State routes — 418, 8 and 74 — either cross it or run beside it. For most of its length, there are also County and Town highways along each bank. However, the character of the river and the density of the vegetation tend to minimize the sense of proximity of these roads. In many places you seem to be in the wilderness.

Accessibility to the river is further enhanced by the excellent access sites established by Warren County and the New York State Department of Environmental Conservation. They are well designed, with turn-arounds and plenty of room for parking. Many of them have inviting picnic areas with fireplaces and trees for shade.

It is possible to start a downriver trip on the Schroon at Sharp Bridge Campsite, a lovely spot covered with large white pines, on US 9 above North Hudson. All the campsites are covered with a carpet of pine needles, and the air is full of their fragrance. A trip begun here would have to be done in the early spring or at a time of heavy runoff. The water has to be high to avoid dragging on the rifts. The stream is about twenty feet wide with an overhang of alder brush and other low-growing trees.

If you are planning a trip on this northern section of the river, be sure to call ahead to find out if the campsite is open. The phone number for the Sharp Bridge Campsite is (518) 532-7538. You can also contact the Department of Environmental Conservation Region 5 Headquarters at Ray Brook, New York 12977, or phone them at (518) 891-1370. There is access at the North Hudson Town swimming area, a park of sorts a mile or so above Frontier Town. The land is not posted, and parking is excellent.

The river winds five and one-half miles down to the North Hudson Bridge, near Exit 29 of I 87. The access here is on the left, or east, bank just above the bridge. Because of the proximity of the popular tourist attraction *Frontier Town*, this is a busy highway, especially during the summer, so park carefully.

This put-in is probably a better starting point for a trip down the Schroon, since the stream at this point is wider and deeper than it is at the Sharp Bridge Campsite and therefore provides canoeing later in the season, depending, of course, on water conditions.

For six miles the river bends and turns, with shallow water riffling over the gravel bottom. At Schroon River hamlet, Johnson Pond Creek comes in on the left. Here the canoer goes under the bridge which carries the highway going west to Blue Ridge, Tahawus and Newcomb. This road goes through some of the pretty back country on the south edge of the High Peaks.

One-quarter mile below the bridge, The Branch, which drains out of Elk Lake, comes in on the right. There is a picturesque waterfall on The Branch about a mile west of the Schroon; it can be seen from the Blue Ridge Road.

Each trip down a river is a new experience. The first time three of my canoeing friends and I went down the Schroon was one of those beautiful balmy May days when the shadblow was still showing and the apple and cherry blossoms were in full bloom. We started early when the morning fog was rising, but soon, as the sun rose higher in the sky, the fog disappeared and the green of the hemlock needles on the banks of the river glistened in the sunlight. Suddenly, we saw something swimming across the stream. A weasel? Mink? It reached the water's edge and scurried up the sloping bank. It stopped and shook the water from its back. At that point we could identify the strange swimmer as a red squirrel. None of us had ever seen a squirrel of any kind swimming in a river. Further downstream a pair of ducks came

Schroon River

Tributary: Hudson River

Counties: Essex, Warren

U.S.G.S. Maps: 15-minute 1/62500
Paradox Lake, Elizabethtown
North Creek, Schroon Lake
7.5-minute 1/24000
Warrensburg, The Glen, Bolton Landing
Brant Lake, Chestertown

Total Length: 65 mi.

Cruising Length: 57 mi.

Season Recommended: April-May

Campsites: Sharp Bridge Public Campsite
Eagle Point Public Campsite
Luzerne Public Campsite
Schroon River Camping Area

Access	Location	Elev. Feet	Distance Miles	Inter. Dist.	Drop Feet	Gradient Ft./Mile	Rating Class
	Source: Ashcraft Pond by Four-Mile Meadow	1,400	65				
	Deadwater Pond	981	60				
A	Sharp Bridge	958	56.8				
				5.5	80	14	I
A	North Hudson Bridge I-87, Exit 29	878	51.3				
				6	48	8	II
A	Schroon Falls, US 9	830	45.3				
				7.9	23	3	II
A	NY 74 Bridge I-87, Exit 28	807	37.4				
				4.6			I
A	Schroon Lake Village I-87, Exit 27	807	32.8				
				3.5			I
A	Eagle Point P.C.	807	29.3				
				1.7			I
A	Horicon Launching Site I-87, Exit 26	807	27.6				
				4.5	7	1	I
A	Starbuckville Bridge	800	23.1				
				7.3	105	15	II-III
A	Riverbank Bridge I-87, Exit 24	695	15.8				
				12.5	27	2	II
A	Warrensburg Access Area	668	3.3				
				3.3	63	20	II-III
A	Jct. Hudson River NY 418 2 mi. W of Warrensburg	605	0				

upriver toward us flying just above the water. We seemed on a collision course until the birds rose abruptly and passed about fifteen feet over our heads. They were the spectacular Common Mergansers, an enjoyable sight on the rivers of the northeast each spring.

An easy paddle of six miles brings you to Schroon Falls where US 9 crosses the river. Schroon Falls drops about four feet and is almost directly under that bridge. To successfully run the falls you need very high water and a closed boat, either a kayak or a closed canoe. You also need considerable skill and maybe a little luck. The prudent route is a portage, taking out on the right bank just above the bridge and putting in about 100 feet down on the same side of the stream.

Below the falls, the river becomes more placid and crisscrosses the valley floor. Because of its meandering course, you may paddle a quarter of a mile but get only a couple of hundred feet closer to Schroon Lake. However, it is such a delightful journey you don't mind the slow progress. Along this calmer stretch, you may see red-winged blackbirds around their nests in the swamp vegetation, or perhaps a family of young turtles sunning themselves on a log amongst the water lilies.

Just below the NY 74 bridge, you will see a take-out. Across the river is a private campground. This egress point is about three miles from the center of the village of Schroon Lake by way of NY 74 and US 9, and is the last take-out before you reach Schroon Lake.

SCHROON LAKE

Schroon Lake is renowned as one of the little gems in the eastern Adirondacks. The village of Schroon Lake is on the west shore near the north end of the lake. There is a public beach here with launching for canoes. The lake is nestled in the hills and is one hundred and fifty-two feet deep; it has a variety of fish, including lake trout, rainbow trout, Atlantic salmon, northern pike and bass. The hamlet of Adirondack is located on the east shore.

There is an abundance of hiking trails in the area, especially in the Pharaoh Lake Wilderness Area, which is located east of the lake. The New York State Department of Environmental Conservation, Albany, New York 12233, has a pamphlet entitled *Trails in the Schroon Lake Region*. For a more complete guide to the region see *Guide to the Eastern Adirondacks*, published by the Adirondack Mountain Club.

Eagle Point Public Campsite is located on the west side at the south

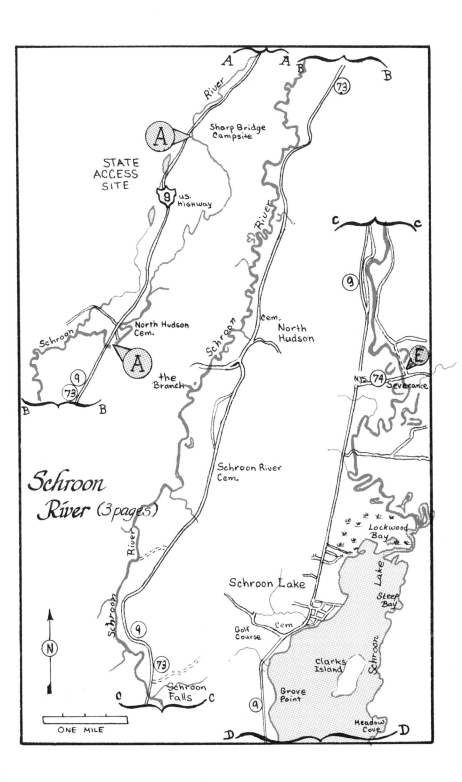

A

STATE
ACCESS
SITE

River

Sharp Bridge
Campsite

A

A

B

73

B

9 U.S.
HIGHWAY

River

C

C

Schroon

North Hudson
Cem.

A

9

73

B   B

the
Branch

Schroon

Cem.
North
Hudson

9

E

N.Y.5. 74
Severance

Schroon River
Cem.

Schroon
River (3 pages)

Schroon

River

Lockwood
Bay

Lake

Schroon Lake

Steep
Bay

N

9

Golf
Course

Cem

Schroon

Clarks
Island

73

Schroon

9

Grove
Point

Meadow
Cove

C   C
Schroon
Falls

D   D

ONE MILE

end of the lake off US 9. There are sixty-eight campsites, a bathing beach, and a launching area.

The State of New York Horicon launching site is on the east shore at the foot (south end) of the lake, near Pottersville. From US 9 you will find directional signs to the launch area.

To canoe the length of Schroon Lake, put in here and go north to the northern end of the lake and up the channel to the DEC access area on NY 74 on the right bank of the river. You may want to reverse the process in order to go south with the current.

LOWER SCHROON

From the outlet of the lake (south end) near Pottersville, the Schroon courses southward. The water is deep and dark and has little current. The New York State *Horicon* launching site is just east of the new bridge on the north side of the County Road that runs east from Pottersville. To save travel time you can put in across the road in a bay below the bridge. Be sure to keep in the main channel so that you don't get lost in one of the several bays which dead end. For a short distance you will see cottages along the right bank, but most of the area adjacent to this section is the huge Jenks Swamp which stretches for about four miles on each side of the stream. The river drops only about an inch every 200 feet here, so you can relax before coming to rougher water.

At Starbuckville four and one-half miles from Horicon, your passage is blocked by a dam. The portage starts on the left bank close to the dam. You can put in the rapids just below the dam, or go further on a well traveled path for about 300 feet and put in on a sandy beach. This spot is another of the excellent Warren County access areas. It has a beautiful white pine grove and is an excellent place to stop for a shore lunch.

It is a leisurely paddle from Starbuckville down to the NY 8 bridge near Exit 25, I-87. Below the bridge, the river gradually picks up speed. About a mile down the stream, you hit some really rough water. If you are an inexperienced paddler you should take out at a little bay on the left — by a big pine stump — about 100 feet above NY 8 bridge. There is another exit on the right bank under the bridge, with a rough trail leading up to the road.

For the intermediate or advanced paddler, the rocky chute — about one-eighth mile long — below the bridge is a real thrill. (At high water it approaches Class III.) Just below these rapids is another Warren County access site on the right bank below the County Road 30 bridge. This one is known as the *South Horicon* access.

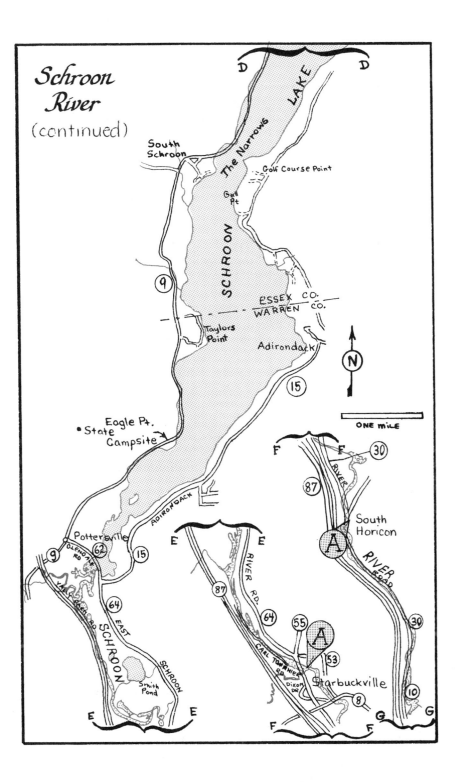

Schroon
River
(continued)

If you weathered the whitewater below the NY 8 bridge, you will be ready for an even more exciting stretch. The river flows southwesterly to a large oxbow, then turns southward. From this point on, be sure your life jacket is on securely, your helmet buckled, and your duffle and extra paddle well secured. Then brace yourself for an exhilarating run.

At medium high or high level, the river rushes down the rocky slope, kicking up haystacks and very choppy water. This is the site of the slalom race sponsored by the Northern New York Paddlers of Schenectady, usually held about the middle of May when the water level is ideal.

After the first steep run, the river slackens its pace. Then for a couple of miles you navigate down through a rocky boulder patch, after which there is a stretch of relatively calm water before you approach the "Big Drop." This should be scouted before running the first time. The river narrows and plunges over a ledge several feet high, then races down through another boulder field and around a bend on the left. After three miles you reach the gauging station steel bridge, from which you coast down to another Warren County access site on the left bank at the foot of a big white pine. The Riverbank Bridge is just beyond it.

Below Riverbank Bridge there are three lively runs before you reach the Schroon River Campsite, a large private campsite on the right bank. There is a driveway that is parallel to and a few feet from the river. In the remaining distance, about eleven miles, to Warrensburg, you can relax and enjoy the foliage and forests interspersed with open fields along the stream banks and view the distant mountains.

On the left bank just below the County Home Road bridge is another fine access. You will recognize it by a red osier dogwood growing at the foot of a large white ash tree, although with ash dieback killing many of our white ash during recent years it is hard to tell how long the tree will be there. About two and one-half miles below this take-out a last surge of the stream carries you under US 9 bridge, and almost immediately the River Street access appears on your left. This is the place to take out if you value your canoe or kayak, although I understand some foolhardy souls run the upper Warrensburg Dam when water conditions are right. I advise against going over the dam under any circumstances.

There is a second dam about a mile below the first. You must portage from the access site to the left bank below the lower dam. It is an easy run from here down to the Hudson River. You can either take out at the junction of the rivers or go on down the Hudson about twelve miles to the take-out on the left bank above the Hadley-Luzerne Falls (a real danger). See Hudson River section for details.

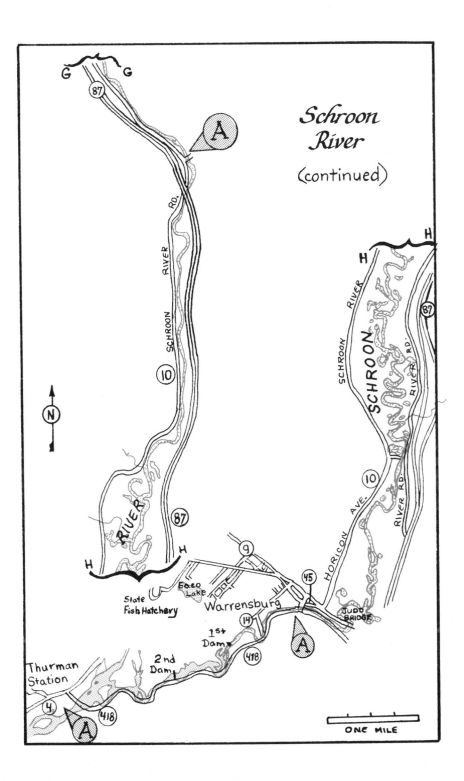

Schroon
River
(continued)

WEST CANADA CREEK

West Canada Creek emerges out of the lakes and bogs of the West Canada Creek Wilderness Area, the highest lake source being Twin Lakes. This is one of the larger wilderness areas of New York State, especially if you include the Moose River Plains. It reaches from NY 8 on the south to NY 28 on the north and takes in a lot of territory in between. It's a thrilling river for canoers. Some people have canoed West Canada Creek from the top, perhaps with regret because of all the obstacles, but that is another story.

To get to the topmost practical spot to begin your trip without trespassing, turn left off NY 8 at Nobleboro and follow up the right or north bank (based on the premise that you are headed for the sea) on the Haskell Road. Drive up the creek about four miles to where the road crosses the stream. Above this the land is privately owned. This is a very rough stream, so inspect it carefully. Don't take any unnecessary chances.

This section of the river can be run only when the water is high, in April and early May. You can call Ed Bielejec at the Mountain Sports Shop in Frankfurt (315-733-5458) to find out if the river is runnable. When the water is four feet high you can expect a fast ride. It is a Class IV stream with the water dropping about sixty feet per mile. Do **not** attempt this run if the water is dangerously high. When you reach the stillwater above the dam at Nobleboro the South Branch of the West Canada Creek comes in on the left. This stream, too, must be done when the water is high.

To reach the starting point for the south branch, drive east on NY 8 about 5 miles from Nobleboro, and turn left onto the Fayle Road. Go four-tenths of a mile to an iron bridge. You can park on the right just before you reach the bridge.

After the stillwater you have a four-mile run of continuous Class II-plus rapids. The stream is narrow—fifty to seventy-five feet—with

West Canada Creek

Tributary: Mohawk River

Counties: Hamilton, Herkimer, Oneida

U.S.G.S. Maps: 7.5-minute 1/24000
Herkimer, Middleville, Newport,
So. Trenton, Remsen, Hinkley
15-minute 1/62500
Ohio, Old Forge, West Canada Lakes

Total Length: 74 mi.

Cruising Length: 46 mi.

Season Recommended:
Upper Section — April-Mid-May;
Hinkley Reservoir — All seasons;
Below Trenton Falls Bridge—
All seasons subject to releases from
reservoir.

Campsites: Pixley Falls Public Campsite

Access	Location	Elev. Feet	Distance Miles	Inter. Dist.	Drop Feet	Gradient Ft./Mile	Rating Class
	Sources:						
	Pillsbury Lake	2,490	74		2,112	29	
	Mud Lake Lean-to	2,345	71				
	Mitchell Dam	2,142	63				
	Swanson Dam	2,078	60				
				12.5	686	55	IV
A	NY 8 Bridge Nobleboro	1,392	48.5				
				8.8	167	19	III
A	McIntosh Bridge	1,225	37.7				
				6.8	2	0	I
E	Hinkley Reservoir	1,223	32.9				
	Prospect Bridge	1,100	30.2		Impassable		
A	Trenton Falls Bridge	740	27.8				
				11	100	9	II
	Newport Dam	640	16.8				
				6.4	86	14	II-III
A	Middleville Bridge	554	10.4				
				6.2	110	18	II-III
A	Kast Bridge	444	4.2				
				4.2	66	15	II
E	Jct. Mohawk R.	378	0				

South Branch

Access	Location	Elev. Feet	Distance Miles	Inter. Dist.	Drop Feet	Gradient Ft./Mile	Rating Class
	Source:						
	T-Lake	2,467	17				
A	Fayle Rd. Bridge	1,624	4.5				
				4.5	230	51	II-III
E	Jct. W. Canada Creek	1,394	0				

trees close in on each side. Keep your eyes open for coyotes and deer; there are plenty of them in this area. This run is a real thriller and ends all too soon for the avid canoer.

From Nobleboro NY 8 bridge the river drops gently forty feet in four miles down to Wilmurt Bridge. Just above the bridge is a horseshoe falls about ten feet high which drops into a deep hole. Portage around the falls on the left bank. About a half-mile below the bridge you enter the Ohio Gorge. The river drops about forty-five feet in one mile, making for some exciting Class III rapids.

From the foot of the gorge to the upper end of six-mile-long Kuyahoora Lake (Hinkley Dam) are three miles with Class II rapids. As you canoe Kuyahoora Lake you will see cottages along its north shore. The south shore is more remote. It is best to take out at the State launching site five-tenths of a mile above the dam on the right bank. A swimming and picnicking area was opened on the south shore in 1984.

Portage from here to the Trenton Falls bridge via NY 365. Turn left onto the Prospect Depot Road just before the overpass. Then take the Prospect Trenton Falls Road down to the bridge below the hydro plant. Park on the right bank where you have a steep access down to the river. You start out through a fast little chute, but the rest of the trip to Newport Dam is quite easy.

Most summers the Trenton Falls Dam is released every day of the week, though in 1983 it was intermittent due to construction. To be sure of conditions I again recommend that you call Ed Bielejec (see above).

The area between Hinkley Dam and the Trenton Falls bridge is great for sightseeing. It is worth a walk to see Trenton Falls, Prospect Falls and the gorge in between.

At Newport Dam take out on the left bank and portage to the foot of the rapids below the bridge. From here on down through Middleville to Kast Bridge there are some great Class II+-III rapids during high water. Some stretches can be scouted from Route 28. About a mile below Kast Bridge there is a dam which you carry around on the right bank. From here on down to the Mohawk River canoeing is easy. The best take-out is at the NY 5 bridge. Otherwise, go down the Mohawk to the next lock and take out on the left bank.

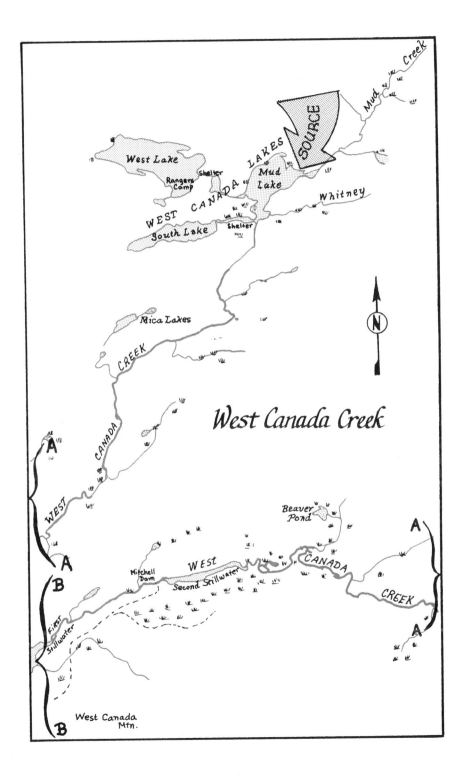

Mud Creek

SOURCE

West Lake

WEST CANADA LAKES

Rangers Camp

Shelter

Mud Lake

Whitney

South Lake

Shelter

Mica Lakes

N

CREEK

WEST CANADA

West Canada Creek

A

Beaver Pond

A

WEST

CANADA

A

B

Mitchell Dam

Second Stillwater

CREEK

First Stillwater

A

West Canada Mtn.

B

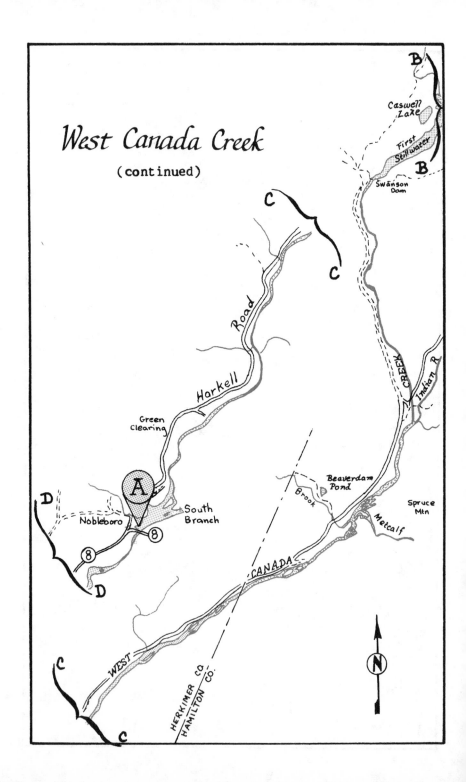

West Canada Creek

(continued)

B

Caswell Lake

First Stillwater

B

Swanson Dam

C

C

Road

Harkell

CREEK

Indian R.

Green Clearing

A

Beaverdam Pond

Brook

Spruce Mtn

D

Nobleboro

South Branch

8

Metcalf

8

D

CANADA

WEST

C

HERKIMER CO.
HAMILTON CO.

C

N

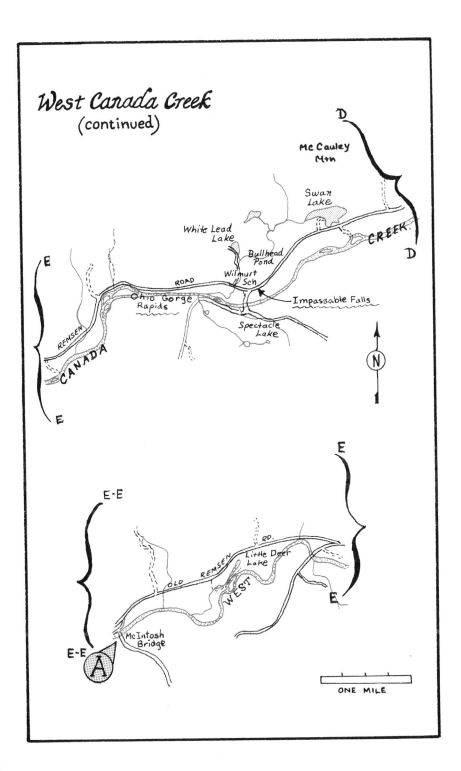

West Canada Creek
(continued)

D

McCauley Mtn

Swan Lake

White Lead Lake

Bullhead Pond

CREEK

D

E

ROAD

Wilmurt Sch

Impassable Falls

REMSEN

Ohio Gorge Rapids

CANADA

Spectacle Lake

E

N

E

E-E

E

Little Deer Lake

RD.

OLD REMSEN

WEST

E

E-E

McIntosh Bridge

A

ONE MILE

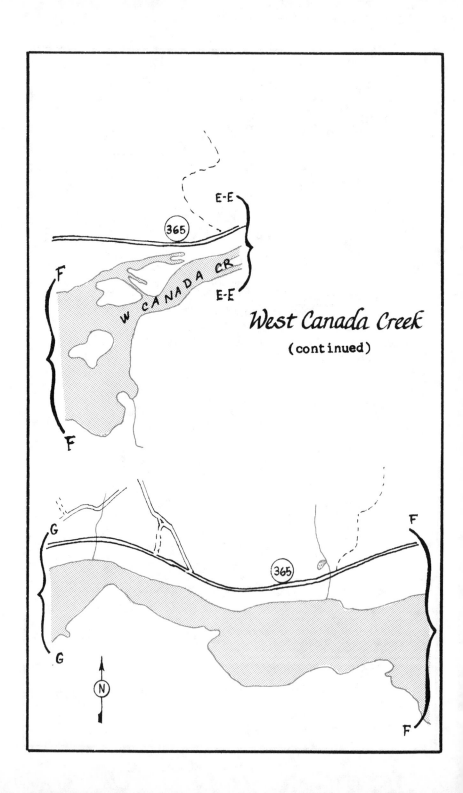

West Canada Creek
(continued)

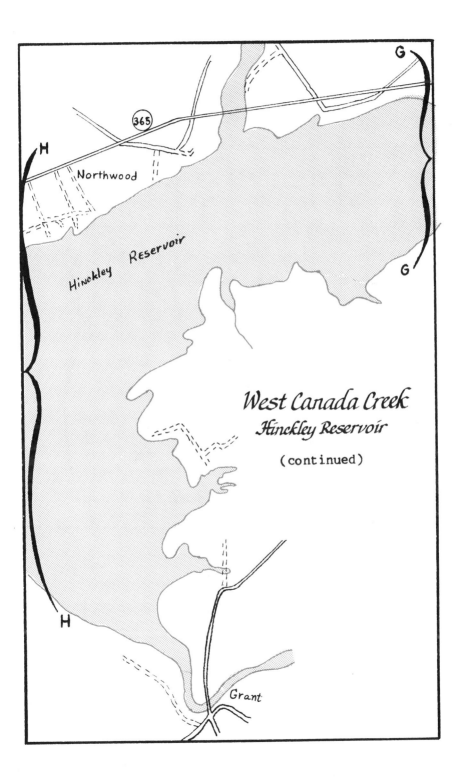

G

365

H

Northwood

Hinckley Reservoir

West Canada Creek
Hinckley Reservoir

(continued)

G

H

Grant

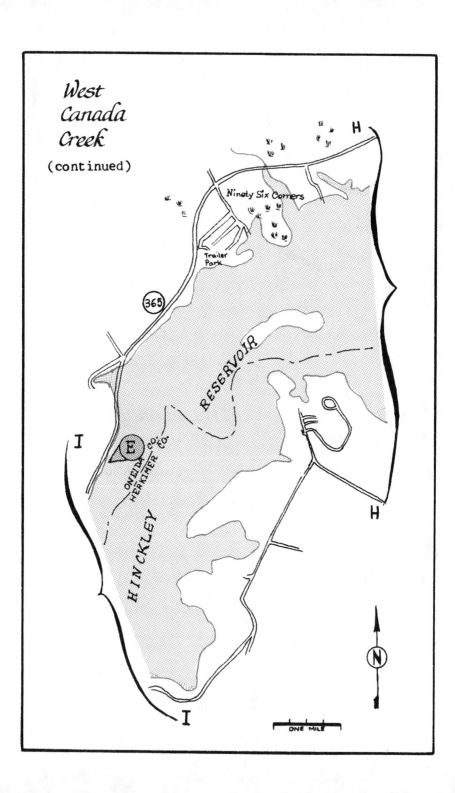

West
Canada
Creek

(continued)

Ninety Six Corners

Trailer
Park

365

RESERVOIR

E

ONEIDA CO.
HERKIMER CO.

HINCKLEY

I

H

H

I

N

ONE MILE

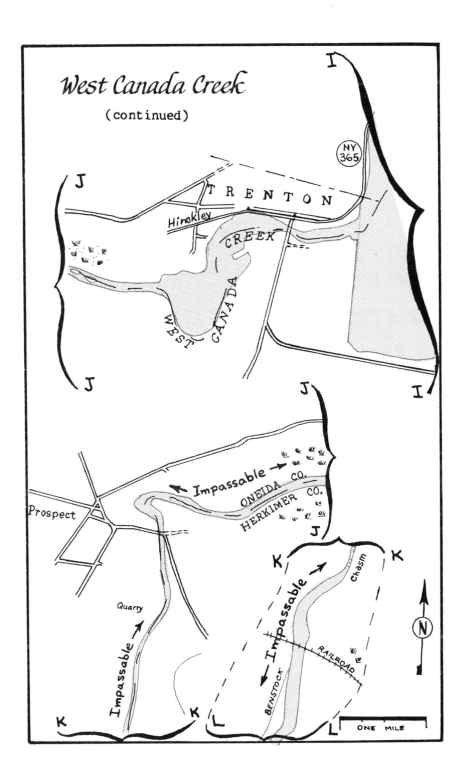

West Canada Creek
(continued)

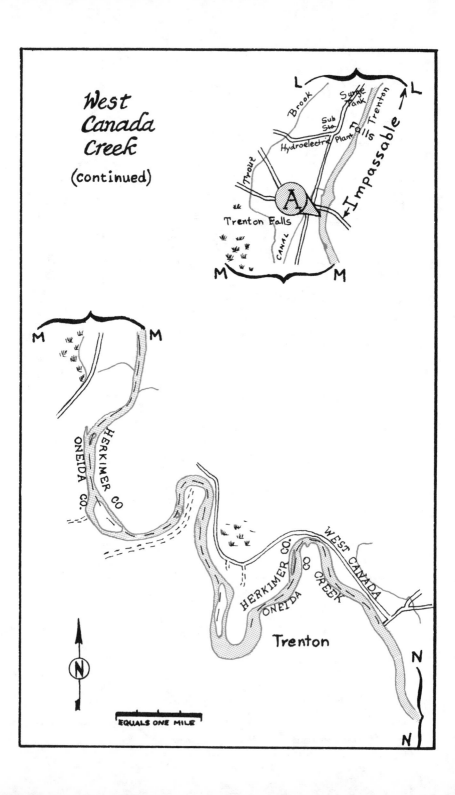

West
Canada
Creek

(continued)

L

Brook
Surge
Tank
Sub
Sta.
Trenton
Hydroelectric Plant
Falls
Trout

Impassable

A

Trenton Falls

CANAL

L

M

M

M

M

HERKIMER CO.

ONEIDA CO.

HERKIMER CO.
ONEIDA CO.

WEST CANADA
CREEK

Trenton

N

N

N

EQUALS ONE MILE

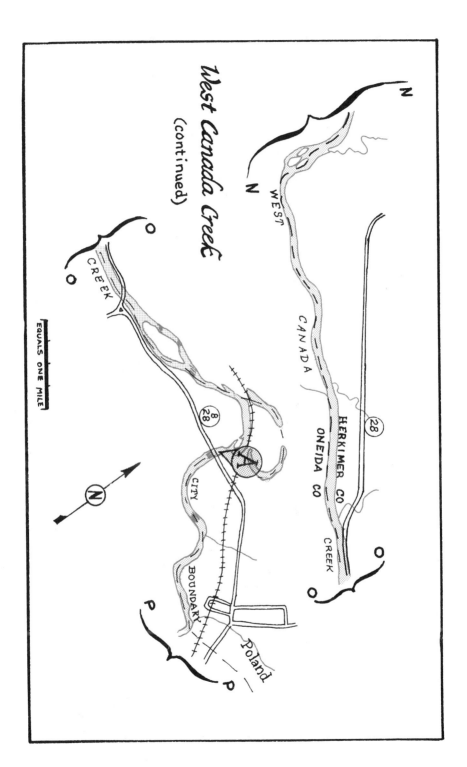

West Canada Creek
(continued)

EQUALS ONE MILE

N

N

WEST

CANADA

ONEIDA CO

HERKIMER CO

CREEK

28

28

O

O

CREEK

N

A

28

CITY

BOUNDARY

Poland

P

P

O

O

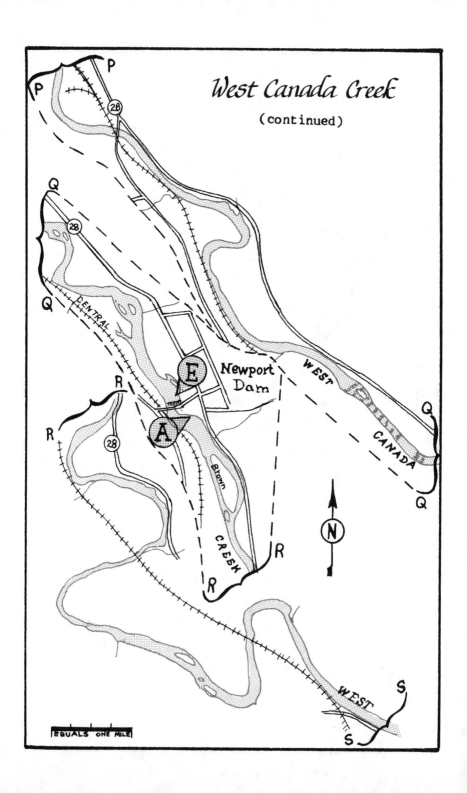

West Canada Creek

(continued)

Newport Dam

EQUALS ONE MILE

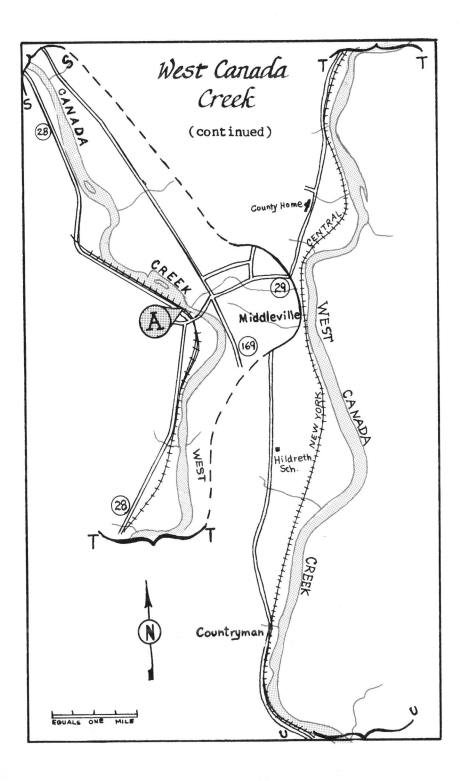

West Canada
Creek

(continued)

County Home

CENTRAL

Middleville

WEST

CANADA

CREEK

NEW YORK

Hildreth
Sch.

Countryman

N

EQUALS ONE MILE

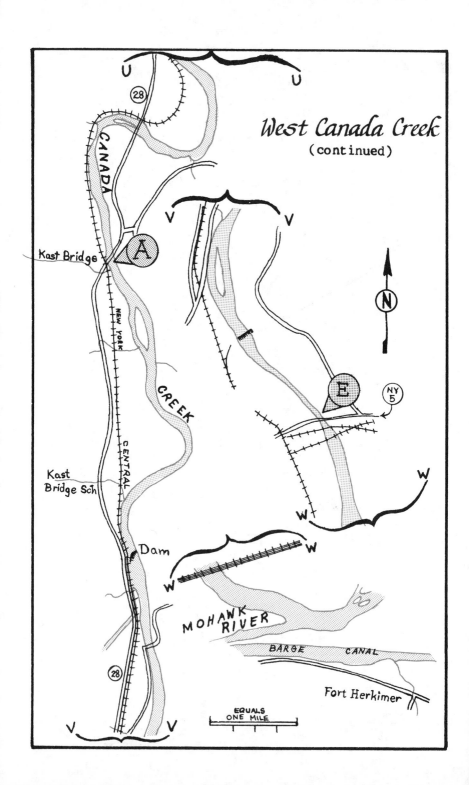

West Canada Creek
(continued)

Kast Bridge

Kast
Bridge Sch

Dam

MOHAWK RIVER

BARGE CANAL

Fort Herkimer

EQUALS
ONE MILE

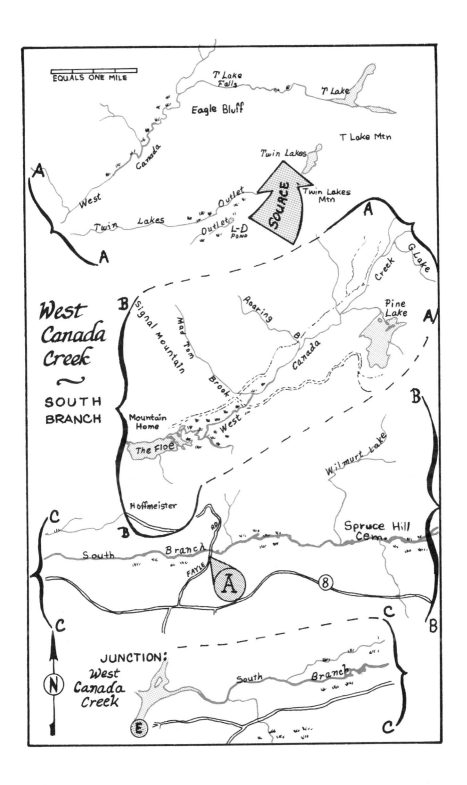

EQUALS ONE MILE

T Lake
Falls

Eagle Bluff

T Lake

T Lake Mtn

Twin Lakes

Source

Twin Lakes
Mtn

A

West

Canada

A

Twin   Lakes

Outlet

Outlet

L-D
Pond

A

Creek

G Lake

*West
Canada
Creek*
~
SOUTH
BRANCH

B

Signal Mountain

Mad Tom

Brook

Roaring

Canada

B

Pine
Lake

A

West

B

Mountain
Home

The Floe

Wilmurt Lake

Hoffmeister

C

B

South   Branch

Spruce Hill
Cem.

FAYLE

(A)

8

C

B

C

JUNCTION:
*West
Canada
Creek*

South   Branch

C

N

(E)

CANOE RACING

Canoe racing has experienced phenomenal growth in this country in the last twenty-five years. While competing in some sports has been described as "barbarian," this is not the case in canoe racing. One of the first rules in canoe racing is if a competitor is in trouble, you stop and help him. Perhaps the greatest benefit to be derived from canoe racing is the development of basic knowledge and techniques. At a race a beginning canoer can look over hundreds of boats, talk with the owners, and watch their performance. You can make intelligent choices about boats and equipment in a short time, and you can learn a great deal about technique by watching the champions do it right.

In the Adirondacks the biggest race is the Hudson River Whitewater Derby, held on the Hudson River at North Creek the first weekend in May. For information write the Hudson River Whitewater Derby Committee at North Creek, N.Y. 12853. The Old Forge Chamber of Commerce can give you information about races on the Moose River and the Fulton Chain of Lakes; the Pulaski Chamber of Commerce about races on the Salmon River. The longest canoe race (seventy miles) in New York State is the General Clinton Race held each Memorial Day on the Susquehanna River. The Bainbridge Chamber of Commerce will send you information about the four-day racing program. The Northern New York Paddlers of Schenectady sponsors an annual race on the Schroon River in the middle of May. There are many other races in the State which are publicized locally.

ORGANIZATIONS

Adirondack Mountain Club
172 Ridge St.
Glens Falls, NY 12801

American Canoe Association
Box 248
Lorton, VA 22079

American Whitewater Affiliation
Box 1261
Jefferson City, MO 65102

American Red Cross
Washington, D.C. 20066

Appalachian Mountain Club
5 Joy Street
Boston, MA 02108

KA-NA-WA-KE Canoe Club
Box 1041
Syracuse, NY 13201

New York Canoe Racing Association
c/o John Ayer
E. Lake Rd.
Skaneateles, NY 13152

Northern New York Paddlers
P.O. Box 228
Schenectady, NY 12301

135

BIBLIOGRAPHY

American Red Cross, *White Water in an Open Canoe, Canoeing,* Washington, D.C.

American White Water Affiliation, *Safety Code,* Jefferson City, MO

Berry, John, *White Water Guide to the Upper Hudson River,* 1976, Riparius, NY

Burmeister, Walter F., *Appalachian Waters 2: The Hudson River and Its Tributaries,* Appalachian Books, Oakton, VA

Gabler, Ray, *New England Whitewater Guide,* Appalachian Mtn. Club, Boston, MA

Grinnell, Lawrence I., *Canoeable Waterways of New York State and Vicinity,* Pageant Press, 1956 (out of print)

Jamieson, Paul F., *Adirondack Canoe Waters, North Flow,* 1981, Adirondack Mountain Club, Glens Falls, NY

KA-NA-WA-KE Canoe Club, *Central New York Canoe Routes,* Syracuse, NY

Miller, Clinton H., Jr., "Three Mines Left in the North Country," *Adirondac,* February 1983.

New York State Department of Environmental Conservation, *Adirondack Canoe Routes,* Albany, NY

Smith, Clyde H., *The Adirondacks,* Viking Press, 1976, New York, NY

U.S. Geological Survey, *Water Resources Data New York Water, Year 1981,* U.S.G.S., Albany, NY

INDEX

access, x
Adirondack Canoe Waters, North Flow, 59
Adirondack Mountain Club, xi, 28, 59
Adirondack trails, 28
Agers Falls, 66
Alger Island, 58
Algonquin Lake, 80
Altmar, 100
American White Water Affiliation, xii
Auger Falls, 78, 80
Austin Falls, 78, 80
Avery Place, 93

Bielejec, Ed, 18, 20, 116
Big Moose Lake, 68, 70
Blue Ledges, 34
Boreas River, 1, 35

campsites, 16, 31, 44, 58, 60, 62, 75, 76, 82, 84, 93, 97, 107, 110
canoe racing, 132
Cedar River, 5, 32, 108
Christine Falls, 78, 80
classifications (ISRD), xviii
clothing, ix
Cunningham, Pat, 32

Department of Environmental Conservation, 100, 107, 108, 110
Department of Transportation, x
drinking water, x

East Canada Creek, ii
egress, x
Elm Lake, 53

Fall Stream, 96
Fish Creek, 18
flow chart, xix
Fulton Chain of Lakes, 54

gauge readings, x
Giardiasis, x
Gooley Club, 31, 32, 34
Great Sacandaga Lake, 76
Griffins Falls, 87
Grinnell, Lawrence, 26

Hadley Luzerne, 36, 42, 114
Harris Lake, 31
Harris Rift, 35
highway markers, x
Hope, 82
Hudson River, 29
Hudson River Gorge, 32
Hudson River White Water Derby, 36, 132

Indian Lake, 44
Indian River, 31, 32, 33, 43
Inlet, 6, 58

Jamieson, Paul, 59
Jessup River, 44

Kunjamuk River, 50, 80
Kunjamuk Cave, 52
Kuyahoora Lake, 118

Lake Pleasant, 50, 76
legend, xix
Lewey Lake, 44

Miami River, 49
Moose River, 54, 132
Moose River Recreation Area, 6, 72

navigation, ix
Newcomb, 27, 32
North Creek, 36, 39, 132
North River, 31, 36
Northville, 82, 84
Northville Placid Trail, 6, 76, 196

137

Old Forge, 54, 58, 59, 64, 132
Oneida Lake, 18
organizations, 133

Pack Forest, 42
Pine Lake, 10
Piseco Lake, 92, 93, 96, 97
Point Rock, 19
Powley Place, 12
Pulaski, 100, 102, 132

Riparius, 39
river difficulty (ratings), xvii

Sacandaga Lake, 76
Sacandaga Public Campsite, 82
Sacandaga River, 50, 76
safety, xii
Salmon River Reservoir, 106
Salmon River, 99
Sanford Lake, 27
Schroon Lake, 110
Schroon River, 42, 107, 143

Shaker Place, 93
signals, xvi
Singing Waters Campground, 60, 62
Speculator, 50, 52, 78, 80
Spring, John B., 10
Spy Lake, 93, 97
Stewart Bridge Reservoir, 80

Taberg, 20
The Glen, 39
Trenton Falls, 118
Tug Hill, 18, 100

U.S.G.S. maps, x
U.S.G.S., xix

Vly Lake, 96

Wakely Dam, 6, 75
Warrensburg, 36, 114
Wells, 80, 94
West Canada Creek, 116
Westdale, 26

NOTES

NOTES